Russia Against Modernity

Russia Against Modernity

ALEXANDER ETKIND

polity

The right of Alexander Etkind to be identified as Author of this Work has
been asserted in accordance with the UK Copyright, Designs and Patents Act
1988.

First published in 2023 by Polity Press

Polity Press
65 Bridge Street
Cambridge CB2 1UR, UK

Polity Press
111 River Street
Hoboken, NJ 07030, USA

ISBN-13: 978-1-5095-5657-1
ISBN-13: 978-1-5095-5658-8(pb)

A catalogue record for this book is available from the British Library.

Library of Congress Control Number: 2022948537

Typeset in 11 on 14pt Warnock Pro
by Cheshire Typesetting Ltd, Cuddington, Cheshire
Printed and bound in Great Britain by TJ Books Ltd, Padstow, Cornwall

The publisher has used its best endeavours to ensure that the URLs for
external websites referred to in this book are correct and active at the time of
going to press. However, the publisher has no responsibility for the websites and
can make no guarantee that a site will remain live or that the content is or will
remain appropriate.

Every effort has been made to trace all copyright holders, but if any have
been overlooked the publisher will be pleased to include any necessary credits in
any subsequent reprint or edition.

For further information on Polity, visit our website:
politybooks.com

Contents

Acknowledgments   vi

Introduction   1
1. Modernity in the Anthropocene   3
2. Petrostate   24
3. Parasitic Governance   40
4. The So-Called Elite   55
5. The Public Sphere   66
6. Gender and Degeneration   85
7. Putin's War   102
8. Defederating Russia   121

Notes   141

Index   160

Acknowledgments

A few decades of observations and debates lie behind this book, but its text was written over several months during the Russian invasion in Ukraine in 2022. I am grateful to the institutions that supported me during those years and months: the European University Institute in Florence; the College of the Future at the University of Konstanz; and the Central European University in Vienna.

John Thompson at Polity Press gave an (almost) unconditional approval to my proposal. Pavel Kolář, Gruia Badescu and Aleida Assmann helped me find the proper words for my thoughts during our discussions in Konstanz. Juliane Furst and several anonymous reviewers read the manuscript and provided invaluable feedback. Dirk Moses and Michael Berdy commissioned me to write articles that I recycled for this book. Tim Clark, John Kennedy, Anatoly Belogorsky and Maria Bratischeva generously helped with criticisms and editing. Mark Etkind, always an inspiration, polished some of my formulations. Several generations of students and friends in St. Petersburg, Cambridge, Lviv, Florence, Riga, Vienna and elsewhere will find here my responses to their questions and objections.

Introduction

This is a lean book about lean modernity and its pompous, archaic enemies. It is a wartime book, and the reader will sense my impatience. However, I started formulating this narrative long before the Russian war in Ukraine resumed in February 2022. The chapters consist of my briefs on Russia's energy, climate action, Covid response, public sphere, demography, gender issues, inequality and war. The last chapter imagines an adventurous though increasingly realistic project of defederating Russia. At the time of writing, the war was not over. Since I was sure it would end at some point, better sooner than later, I decided to write the whole text in the past tense.

I wished this book to be a short and sharp text, a pamphlet rather than a treatise, written with a playfulness that would help the reader grasp its gruesome themes. Peace is good for complexity; war brings clarity. Nothing cleanses the palate better than war. It changes everything – first the present, then the future and, finally, the past. In developing my concept of Russia's "*stop*modernism," I draw on political economy, intellectual history, international relations and much else.

Some of my favorite authors – Alexander Chayanov, John Maynard Keynes, Karl Polanyi, Mikhail Bakhtin and Fernand

Braudel – wrote their greatest books during a major war. Despair is critical – it zooms in on the worst parts of life and brings them to fore where the hidden can be revealed and the invisible analyzed. Compassion for some and contempt for others reduce academic prudence to smoking ashes. Mourning consists of memories, visualizations and speculations: How could this have happened? Could it have been prevented? But this mimesis is also nemesis: How to resist and overcome? What kind of revenge would break a new circle of violence?

Postwar periods are intellectually productive: they create ideas that feed the next generations, though they do not prevent these new generations from starting another war.[1] Postwar periods are good for investors and architects but also for philosophers and historians: shaken by the war, the world must be rebuilt, rebooted and re-anchored all over again. Teaching in Konigsberg when the Russian Empire annexed the city for the first time, Immanuel Kant produced his Critiques of human reason after foreign troops had left his land. Throughout his life, Kant was committed to working towards Perpetual Peace, but Russia refuted his project; few places on the earth have been as distant from peace as Kaliningrad.[2] In 1921 in Strasbourg, another city in the process of changing hands, Marc Bloch discovered the lethal power of lies: "Items of false news . . . have filled the life of humanity . . . False news reports! . . . in every country, at the front as in the rear, we saw them being born and proliferating . . . The old German proverb is relevant: 'When war enters the land, then there are lies like sand.'"[3]

In a desert of lies there are wells of truth that create oases of peace, unless the sand recaptures them. We are the animated pieces of that sand and that water, and the choice between them is ours. This is the story we live in.

1

Modernity in the Anthropocene

Before and during the Russo-Ukrainian War that began in 2014, modernity was as big an issue for Russia as agency was for Ukraine. A harbinger of progress — this was how its sympathizers thought about the Soviet Union, and Putin's Russia wished to be its heir. In 1992, Zygmunt Bauman, a Polish-born sociologist who saw it all, wrote that "communism was modernity's most devout, vigorous and gallant champion . . . It was under communist, not capitalist, auspices that the audacious dream of modernity . . . was pushed to its radical limits: grand designs, unlimited social engineering, huge and bulky technology, total transformation of nature."[1] In this conglomeration of steel, oil and gunpowder, there was very little place for men and women. The all-powerful state subordinated both people and nature to a turbocharged modernity that looked increasingly stagnant, even obsolete, with every passing decade. This was *paleomodernity*, and the Soviet Union was its most vigorous champion.

Argument

Putin's war was a "special operation" against the Ukrainian people, their statehood and culture. It was also a broader operation against the modern world of climate awareness, energy transition and digital labor.

Any concept of modernity comprises descriptive and normative components. The Anthropocene has accelerated their fusion. A new type of modernity – reflexive, sustainable, decentralized – would help us to survive the Anthropocene.[2] Negotiated between the planet and its humans, the new order is very different from the previous types of modernity, such as Max Weber's bureaucratized modernity of the late nineteenth century, or the paleomodernity of the early twentieth. I call it *gaiamodernity*, deriving the name from Gaia, the planetary system of life and matter that includes us all.[3] Paleomodernity defined progress in terms of the expanding use of nature: the more resources were used and the more energy consumed, the higher was a civilization. For gaiamodernity, in contrast, the further advancement of humanity requires less energy used and less matter consumed per every new unit of work and pleasure. The two types of modernity present opposite relations between nature and progress.

Gaia's time is infinite, but it changes with history because we do. In its new condition, humanity will have to overcome the global pollution and corruption that were created by paleomodernity. It will have to abstain from burning fossils and forget about fetishes such as growth. It will have to develop immunities to natural threats. Small is beautiful in this era, whether it is a matter of vehicles, computers or weapons. But this modernity also affirms the vitality of the state, which only grows bigger when faced with natural challenges. We cannot respond to these challenges without the state, and our politics is vital for Gaia.

Unlike the premodern Leviathan, a hypermasculine monster who frightens his people into behaving and producing, the modern state is a part of Gaia: a feminine organism that includes nature and humans in one mammoth body, benevolent but unforgiving. While the purpose of the Leviathan was to halt history for the sake of the ruler, Gaia lives and changes with us, and our history is one. Our society is still a *risk society*, but our state is developing into the new *state of nature*.[4]

Gaiamodernity is real, but not quite; it is also utopian. This modernity is utilitarian, provided that it includes the elements of nature *and* people in its calculus. It is democratic: experts represent nature, but judgment is left up to the people. Most importantly, it is reflexive. Having failed in so many other tasks, we contribute our reflexivity to the life of Gaia.

A taste instead of a plan

Gaiamodernity is both a permanent revolution and a world revolution. Unlike Trotsky, who coined these terms, our leaders have no time for trials and errors. Is this why they are so hesitant to do anything?

Gaiamodernity develops a certain taste, a system of aesthetic preferences, that is very different to that of paleomodernity. Imagine Greta Thunberg conversing with Donald Trump, or Putin talking to Zelensky, both sides harboring an intense repulsion towards the other. While two regimes of modernity meet routinely in the public space, their mutual aversion takes first an aesthetic and only later a political form. Ironically, cultural factors are more consequential in authoritarianism than in democracy. In democratic governance, political choices follow economic and ecological realities, as the people articulate them in their debates and elections. With authoritarians at the helm, it is their idiosyncratic preferences – aesthetic tastes, cultural and sexual prejudices, historical views and ethnic stereotypes – that shape social structuration and dictate the policies of the realm.

With its need for natural resources such as fossil fuel and metal ores, paleomodernity was based on resource colonization, settler imperialism and war capitalism. Valuable resources were always located far away from population centers – this was what made them valuable. New lands had to be occupied, annexed and colonized. The people already living in them were abused, resettled or killed, and new "productive" – or rather, extractive – populations were settled in their place. Seeking raw materials as the basis for its economy and society, paleomodernity had two historical forms, external and internal. The former was created by overseas colonization; the latter was specific to large territorial empires, of which Russia was a perfect example. Internal and external colonization turned into one another with every occupation and annexation, and with every imperial collapse. What was external became internal, and vice versa; the key processes – racism, genocide, exploitation, creolization – were the same.[5]

Gaiamodernity turns the legacy of paleomodernity on its head. Progress should be green and safe, sustainable and decentralized. Using renewable energy, autonomous *prosumers* will abolish their feudal dependency on distant deserts and marshes. The new modernity will eschew the transportation routes that were the darlings of paleomodernity. With no pipelines or tankers to feed us there will be fewer pirates and terrorists to harm us, and fewer security experts to exercise control over us. This utopian modernity will differentiate between public goods and public bads, which were stuck together in paleomodern society. Cherishing anthropological diversity – racial, sexual and intellectual – the new modernity will abhor monopolies and oligarchies. It will digitalize education and entertainment, saving materials and emissions by going online. Gaiamodernity will be cosmopolitan: it will not profit from globalization but will work for the good of everyone because, as in certain Gnostic heresies, either all will be saved or all will perish. Gaiamodernity is a utopia in the making. We are living through its birth pangs, and history is accelerating.

But there are many who wish to protect their old habits and treasure, and they have launched their counter-offensives. The Russian invasion of Ukraine was one of these. The growing awareness of climate change and social inequality was the real threat to Putin's oil-fed officialdom. This mixed group of "oiligarchs" and bureaucrats perceived the advance of history as an existential threat: it would damage the oil and gas trade, depriving Russia of its main source of income; it would rob Russia of the unique advantages it would supposedly gain from climate change; and it would introduce "unpredictability" into the established, and highly unequal, social and gender order.

The Russian state confronted modernity by drilling for oil and gas, occupying foreign countries, accumulating gold, subsidizing far-right movements around the world, and destroying Ukraine. Its politics was not inertial but the opposite – active, even proactive, determination. Russia's demodernization was an intentional activity, a mode of structuration that was freely chosen by the Russian elite and imposed upon the broader population, and subsequently upon the global arena.[6] Russia had some allies in this venture, but the project of reversing modernity was its own "special operation": stopmodernism.

Demonstrating an unexpected focus and creativity, the Kremlin used various strategies to resist and reverse gaiamodernity, from climate denialism to electoral interference to war. There was no secret, long-term plan that coordinated these efforts in advance. Anthony Giddens's theory of structuration provides a better perspective: agency creates structures that modify the opportunities for a new action, and this action changes the underlying structures that open or close the new opportunities.[7] Instead of a master plan for future change, the ruling group had preferences that defined its choices at every step: *a taste rather than a plan.*

Russia's all-out war against Ukraine and the world turned its slow, hesitant demodernization into a disruptive campaign against modernity. Prepared in secrecy but known to the American and British intelligence services, the invasion shocked the vast majority of Russian, Ukrainian and European intellectuals. Even in January 2022, my friends and colleagues both in Russia and Ukraine considered the chances of invasion negligible, and the very idea laughable. Nobody expected this war to happen, wrote Masha Gessen, who visited both Moscow and Kyiv on the eve of the invasion: "The prospect of war was literally unbelievable. It continued to be unimaginable, unthinkable even after it began."[8] But the invasion did happen. Different people live in different worlds, each of them integrated by various forces of cohesion – psychological, aesthetic and political. These worlds clash with the outbreak of a war – a shock for some, a triumph for others, and hard work for everyone who must restructure their subjective lifeworlds.

Starting the war was a deliberate decision of a kind that Carl Schmitt, the Kremlin's half-acknowledged guide in political theory, deemed essential for political practice. The war did not follow from any rational calculus that existed in the past, and it changed the grounds for all such calculations in the future. The actions of certain people and institutions defined the life, work or death of millions of other people.[9] This is structuration in practice. Agents create structures that shape new actions, and these agents themselves change in the process. They may or may not have a plan; and if they have one they may not follow it. But in making such decisions, agents follow their tastes, which stabilize with each decision. In this way, aesthetic and cultural preferences enter the political realm, shape economic relations and drive history.

Trust

Modern nations evolve in a delicate balance between civil society and the state.[10] There is a subjective mood that holds them together: trust. It is a feeling, a sentiment, that underlies structural formations. As German sociologist Niklas Luhmann aptly remarked: "A complete absence of trust would prevent [one] even getting up in the morning."[11] Both before and during the war, millions of Russians had this feeling that spoiled their mornings, and evenings as well. An absence of trust destroys an individual; when it affects many people, it destroys their society. Breakdowns of trust are abrupt and catastrophic, and they are known as revolutions.

Trust can be imposed by an all-powerful state: historians of Russia speak of forced or imitated trust.[12] But if this state is in decline, your only choice is between silence and protest. Real change can take decades, and nothing but corruption and emissions would be produced during this period. "The expectation of catastrophes undermines trust," wrote Ulrich Beck.[13]

For paleomodernity, the main example of trust was credit: multiple borrowers were equally related to a lender, and mutual trust was about individual responsibility. For gaiamodernity, trust is about sorted garbage, clean water and a peaceful country. People can only achieve this together, through their coordinated efforts. It is a collective responsibility that involves the authorities as well as citizens. Dealing with pollution, pandemic, or dictatorship, people again live in the state of nature as if they were in Hobbes's old fantasy, but this time it is really about the state *and* nature.

Our situation is close to that of new wilderness, in which trust is dispersed and selective. Trust your friends and test them; hate your enemies. Remember postmodernism, in which all cultural things were said to be equal? It was a lie – the real threat is stopmodernism. But its features are not yet clear, or at least they were not clear before the war. This is the time for a new reflexivity. No more blind trust: the risks are calculable, as are the countermeasures. Trust your neighbor not to pollute your air, or spread the virus any more than is inevitable; but always check just in case. And trust your authorities in the same way. It is their duty to protect you. If they produce more emissions rather than less, then they should go. This is the time for a new moral autonomy. Trust yourself, and you will get up in the morning.

To survive the Anthropocene we have to trust the experts. We live in a world of probabilities that we cannot perceive. It is the experts who tell us about climate change, viruses, pollution and other challenges. Rarely can we test their data, but we are eager to discuss their conclusions and recommendations. This is how the public sphere, a crucial mechanism of gaiamodernity, works. Distrust splits the public sphere into fragments that refuse to communicate with one another. It creates a cultural gap between the commoners on the one hand, and the experts and authorities on the other. Commoners do not trust them and do not comply; sabotage, the weapon of last resort, is not as weak as it seems. In many situations, distrust works as a self-fulfilling prophecy. You feel that sorting your rubbish isn't worthwhile, so you don't do it. The unsorted garbage ends up in the same place as the sorted, confirming your indifference to the issue. If you do not get a jab the world will not end either. You may get sick or die, but only the experts will know why.

This cultural gap between the elite and the commoners never stays empty. The folk fill it with immaterial subtleties – popular culture (Mikhail Bakhtin), hidden transcripts (James Scott) or conspiracy theories, as we now call them. If the experts are too distant, the elite too arrogant, and the gap too great, conspiracy theories tend to materialize in a self-fulfilling manner. Russia's corruption, inequality and bad governance converged in the destruction of social trust.[14] Tragically, this effect reached a climax at exactly the point when trust was more important than ever: on the eve of the Covid-19 pandemic, in the context of the global decarbonization, and during the undeclared war.

Putinism in Eurasia

Putin's aim was to restore the Soviet-style paleomodernity – the reign of oil, steel and smoke, the majesty of military power, the coerced unity of the people. The Soviet Union based its power and glory on socialism – an ideal of brotherhood and the equality of all. Although it failed to materialize, this ideal was relatively effective in containing corruption. Putin and his people wished to combine the Soviet allure with post-Soviet graft. Their reenactment of paleomodernity merged legacies from the Soviet era – resource waste, cynicism and distrust – with the radical novelty of massive and ever-increasing inequality. Ulrich Beck wrote that "social inequalities and climate change are two sides of the same coin";[15] resistance to them also had one and the same origin. Confronting these two major challenges – climate and inequality – the Kremlin sang to the tune of libertarian, denialist conservatism. Imitating or reinventing this ideology, the Russian rulers supported far-right movements around the world.

Russia's environmental problems were immense. The Global North and the Arctic proved to be even more vulnerable to climate change than the South. In 1991, permafrost covered two thirds of the Russian territory, but has been in retreat ever since. Cities, pipelines and railways sat on this melting land.[16] Collapsing randomly, the permafrost released enormous amounts of methane, which accelerated global warming. In 2021, almost twenty million hectares of Siberian forest were destroyed by wildfires; it was Russia's most destructive wildfire season ever. From the tundra to the taiga, Siberian ecosystems were changing from being carbon sinks to being active emitters. In terms of its vulnerability to climate crisis, Russia was comparable to Canada and Alaska; but only in Russia did major cities such as Yakutsk and Norilsk sit on melting permafrost.

The war and sanctions of 2022 increased the flaring of natural gas, a major source of pollution. Symbolic of the excess characteristic of the oil and gas trade, the flaring was ubiquitous: since it was difficult to shut down gas wells or preserve the gas, the only way to get rid of the excess was to burn it off into the air. The less gas the Russian corporations were able to sell the more they flared on the spot or somewhere along the line. In August 2022, just one Russian compressor station near the Finnish border was burning ten million dollars worth of Siberian gas every day.[17] In the way of nemesis, this added to the local pollution around St. Petersburg, Putin's native city, before it contributed to global emissions.

Watching the Siberian fires, the retreat of the permafrost and the massive release of methane, Putinism blessed Russia's role as an energy empire. Insisting that oil and gas exports were essential for the national economy, experts speculated on the possible benefits of climate change for Russia.[18] As a northern country with an unstable agriculture, would it not be better for the country to be a little warmer? Wouldn't the opening of the Northern Sea Route to China realize the ancient dreams of Ivan the Terrible? Along with climate denialism, other components of Putinism included cultural conservatism, homophobia, economic inequality and graft. They were all connected.[19] In July 2022, Putin explained the energy transition underway in European countries by their "love of non-traditional relations," a Russian euphemism for homosexuality; here, climate denialism merged smoothly with homophobia.[20] Machismo was a persistent feature of Putin's speeches; in August that year, he said that only masculinity could protect the governments of the world from the designs of American imperialism.[21]

Putinism emphasized its continuity with Soviet-style socialism, but it could not combine its libertarian policies with any version of left ideology. Perceptive scholars saw that Putinism was moving towards fascism, but social disparities prevented its development into a mass movement.[22] If Putinism had an ideology it was imperialism in its special form of revanchism. Although nationalist at its core, Putinism was also an international movement; from its financial and political base in Russia, it spread around the world. Before the war, Putin and his people maintained a balance between their ultra-conservative message and their revisionist stance, which was digestible only for their Russian supporters. The war demonstrated the fragility of this alliance. Post-Soviet revanchism meant nothing to Putin's international allies. Even the US Republican Party, a loyal partner of Moscow for decades, condemned the invasion in Ukraine.

Economically, Putinism focused on Russia's energy exports. The Kremlin was the main beneficiary of supply chains that started in the Siberian marshes and ended in European and Asian fuel tanks, boilers and air-conditioners. In the era of climate crisis and inequality concerns, the Kremlin wished to conceal both its dependency on fossil trade and the damage it was doing to the planet. The Russian government produced three responses to the growing awareness of climate change: denial, deception and military preparations.

Denial

Three decades of boom and bust in post-Soviet Russia coincided with its long and tortured cognizance of the climate crisis. The Soviet Union collapsed in 1991, giving life to fifteen independent states, Russia and Ukraine among them. In 1992, the United Nations adopted its Convention on Climate Change, which acknowledged "dangerous human interference with the climate system." That year, Putin was working in St. Petersburg, where he controlled foreign trade and got his first taste of corruption. Adopted in 1997, the Kyoto Protocol created the first international mechanism for controlling emissions. In 1998, miners' strikes and a financial crisis brought Russia to default; in the midst of this turmoil, Putin was appointed head of the Federal Security Service, his powerbase for decades to come. In 2000, Paul Crutzen, the Nobel Prize-winning chemist, coined the concept of the Anthropocene, and Putin became Russia's president. In 2004, Rex Tillerson, an engineer from Texas who specialized in Russian oil, became the head of ExxonMobil. That same year, the Orange Revolution started in Kyiv. In 2005, ExxonMobil and the Koch brothers launched a massive campaign of climate denial in the American media. In 2008, Putin swapped roles with his adjutant Dmitry Medvedev, who formulated a vague program of modernization. In 2012, Putin returned to the Kremlin amid protests in Moscow. Between 2009 and 2011, "Climategate" attempted to discredit the scientific research on climate change. In 2014, the Revolution of Dignity in Kyiv paved the way for the European development of Ukraine. That year, Putin occupied and annexed Crimea. In 2015, the Paris Climate Agreement was struck. Supported by Putin, Donald Trump became President of the United States in 2016 and appointed Rex Tillerson as his Secretary of State. The US withdrew from the Paris Treaty in 2017. The global Covid-19 pandemic began in China in December 2019, with Russia suffering the highest excess mortality worldwide. In 2020, the EU adopted the European Green Deal, an ambitious program for halving its emissions. In 2022, Russia ramped up its war against Ukraine.

The burning of fossil fuels created the CO_2 emissions that led to climate crisis. The truth was as simple as that, but there were vested interests in denying it. Russia was a major exporter of oil, gas and coal. Climate awareness threatened its existential interests, as Putin's experts well understood. A great source for studying Russia's climate denialism are the writings of Andrei Illarionov, economic advisor to President Putin from 2000 to 2005, and later a senior fellow at the Cato Institute,

Washington DC. Having written volumes of analytics that denied the manmade character of climate change, Illarionov stated in 2004 that the Kyoto Protocol was something like an "international Gosplan" (referring to the USSR's State Planning Committee), only much worse. In fact, he said, "the Kyoto Protocol is akin to the Gulag and Auschwitz." What's the connection? – Kyoto was "a treaty of death ... since its main goal is to stifle economic growth and economic activity in the countries that will accept the obligations of this protocol."[23] Illarionov's position was close to that of many in the Russian elite.

In 2009, the unknown hackers who initiated Climategate stole and published thousands of private emails in the hope of demonstrating that climate change was a scientific conspiracy. Two years later, a Russian server published yet another trove of 5,000 climate-related emails. These cyberattacks on climate science prefigured the larger operations that defined the politics of the following decade. Illarionov was later an avid supporter of Donald Trump. In 2021, he was fired from the Cato Institute because of his allegations that the attack on the US Capitol was a "trap" set by police. In multiple interviews, he denied Russia's military preparations right up until the invasion of Ukraine. The Cato Institute, a libertarian thinktank financed by the Koch brothers, was an intellectual center of the global climate-denial movement. The father of these brothers, Fred Koch, was also the father of the Soviet oil-refining industry. Having invented new ways of cracking oil, Koch built fifteen refineries in the Soviet Union between 1929 and 1932. Before his eyes, his friends and associates were arrested and murdered during the Soviet terror.[24] Disenchanted like many other fellow-travelers, Koch turned into an avid enemy of the international left; I call it the Ayn Rand syndrome.[25] Eventually, Koch returned his business to the US, though he also helped to build refineries for Nazi Germany. His heirs, Charles and David Koch, the owners of the biggest petrochemical company in the US, ambivalently

supported Trump's candidacy in 2016. But their real interest
was the fusion of libertarianism and climate denialism that was
so characteristic of Putinism.

For the global efforts at climate action, Russia's denialism was a strategic obstacle. Euro-Atlantic leaders imagined
decarbonization as a process of cooperation and shared
sacrifice. Many of them also had doubts and fears regarding
decarbonization. But only the beneficiaries of the oil and gas
trade knew precisely how much they would lose if this trade
were to cease. The truth was that sellers of carbon would
suffer more than its buyers. For various reasons, state actors
and climate activists underestimated this structural asymmetry. With some naivety, they thought that climate awareness
would be equal at all nodes of the fossil trade. But Russia's
absence from the climate deal turned the common cause into
a zero-sum game.

Deception

In the 2010s, the climate crisis was developing rapidly. Heat
waves, extreme weather events, fires and famines proved its
existence to voters across the world. In Europe and other
continents, democratic governments felt obliged to show their
awareness of the crisis but largely failed to coordinate their
actions. Drilling and petrochemical corporations spent billions
on lobbying to block any meaningful decarbonization policies.

During this period, climate action took neoliberal forms
which were amenable to the Russian rulers: as a big country
with a low population density, Russia could gain from the new
trading schemes. In 2009, the Russian government issued the
Climate Doctrine, which acknowledged the manmade character of climate change. At the Copenhagen Climate Conference
of that year, President Medvedev promised to increase Russian
energy efficiency by 40 percent. But the conference ended in

chaos, and Medvedev's program of modernization was not fulfilled.

A real decarbonization has never been on the Kremlin agenda. The collapse of the USSR and the decline of Russia's economy had reduced emissions within its territory without any effort on the part of its rulers. In 2013, the Kremlin set a national target to reduce emissions to 75 percent of the 1990 rate; while this sounded ambitious, in fact Russia's emissions were already less than 70 percent of that rate.[26] The Russian rulers survived the deindustrialization of their country only by the increasing the volume of its carbon exports. Since the exported oil, gas and coal were burned in other countries, the resulting emissions were somebody else's problem. As Russian emissions would be seen to decrease while global emissions continued to rise, Europe, China and the rest of the world would have to pay emission transfers to Russia. But few wanted to pay twice for their fuel.

In 2015, Sergey Donskoy, minister of natural resources, estimated potential Russian losses from climate change at 1–2 percent of GDP per year.[27] However, the proportion of Russian GDP made up by the oil, gas and coal trades was much higher, at 15–25 percent a year. Unlike the rest of its GDP, which was the result of the hard work of Russian citizens and partially returned to them in salaries and pensions, the carbon revenue directly enriched the government. A real decarbonization program adopted by the European and global economies would eliminate these state profits – the source of the Kremlin's official expenditures as well as its subterranean corruption. In 2016, new hacks and leaks from Russia helped to elect Donald Trump, the climate denier in chief. In 2018, at the Katowice Climate Change Conference, Trump's America, Putin's Russia, Saudi Arabia and Kuwait blocked the adoption of a binding resolution.

Year after year, fossil fuels made up more than two-thirds of Russia's exports and funded more than half of its federal budget. The lion's share of this funding came from Europe, which in 2021 bought three-quarters of Russia's gas exports and two-thirds of its oil exports. The money was crucial for the stability of Russia's currency, for its military spending, for maintaining the luxurious lifestyle of its elite, and for importing consumer goods for the general population. For the EU, Russian exports provided about 40 percent of its gas, about half of its coal and a quarter of its oil. The relationship was symbiotic, though Russia depended on it more than Europe. The EU's planned energy transition would mean a replacement of products extracted from nature with goods created by labor. This would result in a major reduction of Russian profits. Despite all the talk of modernization and diversification, there was no plan for substituting Russia's fossil fuel exports with any other source of revenue. And if there were hopes of cheating the planet through the EU Trading Emissions Scheme (2009), there would be no way around the EU Transborder Carbon Tax (2021).

Planned for implementation in 2026, the Carbon Tax would impact the cost of all high-carbon products, including steel, cement, aluminum and petrochemicals. Non-EU producers of these commodities would pay €75 per metric ton of emissions occurring during the production of them. The effect on Russian exports would be equivalent to an additional customs charge of 16 percent.[28] In April 2021, the EU declared its commitment to reducing emissions by half by 2030 and to zero by 2050. This would mean proportional reductions of oil and coal purchases. Gas, a cleaner fuel, would keep flowing for another decade. "You see what is happening in Europe. There is hysteria and confusion in the markets," said Putin in October 2021.[29] By this point, Russian war preparations were in full swing.

Normalization

"Russia is a normal country" was the slogan of a whole generation of Western experts. The Cold War had been settled, and
academic interests switched to the Third World. The liberal left
presented Russia as a decent partner and a reliable counter-
weight to the United States. A neoliberal idea of normalization
colored studies in the history, sociology and politics of Russia:
if an empirical work needed an ideological impetus, the notion
of normalization provided it. A good example is an essay by
two leading American scholars, an economist and a political
scientist, "A Normal Country: Russia after Communism," published in 2005, right after the Orange Revolution in Ukraine.[30]
I could cite hundreds of other examples. The normalization of
Russia was a massive and high-profile endeavor, an intellectual
equivalent of the Marshall Plan. For many observers, it was
only Russia's genocidal war with Ukraine that changed this
understanding.

In 2012, the World Bank upgraded Russia to a high-income
economy but reversed this decision two years later.[31] Average
Russian incomes had been falling since 2012, which happened
in very few other countries. In terms of median incomes,
Russia ranked 46th in 2021 – lower than Lebanon or Bulgaria.
For that same year, the Harvard Atlas of Economic Complexity
ranked Russia 51st, between India and Vietnam, and far lower
than its geographic neighbors Finland and China.[32] Health
spending per capita was even worse: 104th place, on par with
Nigeria and Uzbekistan. Predictably, Russia's ranking for life
expectancy was similar: 105th. Underspending on education was gruesome: though a richer country, Russia spent
less per capita on education than Turkey, Mexico or Latvia.
When measured on the portion of GDP spent on educational
institutions, Russia ranked 125th.[33] Russia's ranking on the
Freedom of Press Index was pathetic from the outset (121st in
2002), and has only got worse since. It ranked 148th in 2020,

between Palestine and Burma, and 158th in 2022, alongside Afghanistan.[34]

Ecologically, Russia was the fourth greatest polluter in the world; China topped the list but Russian emissions per capita were much higher.[35] Russia's ecological problems – smog in the capital and garbage in the countryside – stuck in the mind of anyone who had visited the country. Siberia had been extensively logged and ravaged by fires. Flaring gas torches and methane leaks created massive emissions. The biggest protest Russia saw during the 2010s was sparked by a plan to ship millions of tons of residential waste from Moscow to the pine forests of the Archangelsk region.

It was no wonder, then, that Russians were so unhappy: in 2020, one global happiness index placed Russia 78th, between the silent Turkmenistan and the protesting Hong Kong.[36] Russia was among those countries with the highest rates of suicide, fatal road accidents and industrial accidents. All these contributed to Russia's pathetic performance in population growth, which reflects rates of fertility, health and migration: 178th, very close to the bottom.[37] Finally, in the World Bank rating of political stability, Russia ranked 147th in 2020, between Belarus and Papua New Guinea.[38] More recent estimates are not available, but my guess is that they would be off the chart.

How was it possible that the well-educated people of this rich country were so poor and unfree? Where did Russian money come from and where did it vanish to? Why did such an enormous country with a long history and famous technological advances make its people so unhappy and unhealthy? The answer is simple: the Russian state. It was huge, archaic and very expensive (see Chapter 3). Moreover, it did not rely on the people but was wholly dependent on the exploitation of natural resources, and mostly one type of them: fossil fuels. Competing with the United States and Saudi Arabia, Russia belonged to the *troika* that led the world in oil extraction.

Russia was also the biggest exporter of natural gas worldwide, and the sixth largest producer of coal, after China and others. If one summed up all these carbon calories, Russia would top the world rankings. But while the US and China consumed the majority of their fossil fuels domestically, Russia was the world's leading exporter of energy. Taking into account wherever its fossil fuels were delivered and burned, Russia was responsible for more emissions than any other country in the world except the US.[39] As a result, by selling as much oil and gas as Saudi Arabia and Qatar *combined*, Russia was a very rich country indeed.

Russia's military expenditure between 2000 and 2020 exceeded a trillion dollars.[40] This was an enormous sum of money, but it represented a minor portion of Russia's oil and gas profits. Taken together, the country's military, security and law-enforcement costs were equal to a third of federal expenditure; in addition, one fifth of the budget remained secret, which was unparalleled in modern economies.[41] During these two decades, Russia's military budget increased by a factor of seven, compared to a factor of two in Germany and 2.5 in the United States. At the start of its invasion of Ukraine, Russia spent about one billion dollars a day on its war effort, depleting its annual military budget within a couple of months. The Russian economy was half the size of Germany's, despite the fact that its population was almost twice as big; but Russia's military budget was much higher than Germany's. With a population smaller than Brazil's, Russia had a much larger standing army. Though it had a GDP inferior to that of the US by a factor of seven, Russia nevertheless competed with the US for military predominance. Early twenty-first-century Russia was the most unequal, the most militarized and the most carbonized among the big countries of the world. Under Putin's rule, it became the most unpredictable of them all.

Saving money on social spending – health care, education, pensions and urban development – the Russian rulers cultivated a mutual understanding with right-wing Republicans in the US, who were also dependent on oil money. In fact, however, Putin's overblown and aggressive state was the exact opposite of the Tea Party ideal. As a ruler, Putin was much closer to the pompous and erratic King George III than to the Boston protesters who threw tea chests into the sea. From King George to Putin, mercantilist dictators wished to see their treasuries enriched and their subjects impoverished.

For classical economics, it was the labor of citizens that constituted the source of a country's wealth. This idea was at the core of the labor theory of value, developed by Adam Smith and Karl Marx, and it continues to feature in contemporary economics textbooks. It was not true, however, that labor alone produced value. Imperial states such as England and Belgium derived enormous wealth and power from the natural resources they shipped from colonies both near and distant.[42] But even in this imperial context, Russia was an anomaly. There, a combination of neomercantilism, internal colonization, libertarian taxes and uncontrolled corruption created one of the most unequal, top-heavy societies in history (see Chapter 4).

During three long post-Soviet decades, Russia had an excellent chance to reshape itself into a peaceful, law-abiding and hard-working country. But its massive security apparatus and corrupt, irrational bureaucracy mopped up the wealth produced from holes in the earth rather than by the work of the people. This greedy "elite" drew almost all of its lifeblood from the sale of fossil fuels, rendering the population redundant for its purposes. Sometimes, however, and particularly in times of crisis, this large and needy population became a nuisance, and potentially a danger. The crowds of protestors who took to the streets of Moscow in 2012 were as threatening to Putin and his regime as the Ukrainian troops of 2022, though the latter were much more deadly, albeit more distant.

The Russian attack on Ukraine was one battle in the larger war of the Anthropocene. Any war is a mega-polluter, and there should be no war in the age of climate crisis. Russian tanks and missiles were bringing an end not only to human lives but, potentially, to human life itself.

2

Petrostate

Historically, the concepts of climate change and the petrostate developed in parallel but independently of one another. Both were introduced in the early 1980s. While the climate crisis has been acknowledged as a global issue and a common destiny, the petrostate has been understood as the local problem of a few distant countries, all of them rogue but also indispensable for the global economy. The best study of the petrostate is that of the Venezuelan anthropologist Fernando Coronil, in his 1997 book *The Magical State.*[1] A little later, the South American world gave us another helpful concept, *extractivismo.*[2] Political scientists preferred the notion of "oil curse," but they applied it exclusively to the Third World. For the carbon-dependent countries of the First World, there was the concept of "Dutch disease," which was favored by economists. Despite semantic differences, all these nation-specific concepts reflected a larger malaise that was destroying the whole human world. At this global level, the problem is called the Anthropocene. Extracted from the depths of the earth, oil first pollutes the immediate environment, then corrupts the polity it enriches, and finally poisons the Earth's atmosphere. As I wrote in another book, we will never run out of oil because we will run out of air first.[3]

Extraction vs. production

Russia's booms and busts followed the inflows and outflows of petrodollars and gas-euros. This was not unique, but rather exemplary. Due to its geographic scale and military might, Russia amplified the typical problems of many oil-extracting states, from Venezuela to Saudi Arabia. But the oil curse played a particularly vicious role in Russia precisely because it had a large and educated population.

Only 1 percent of the Russian population worked in the fossil fuel extraction and transportation industry, and a much smaller group benefited from it. However, this trade accounted for more than half of Russia's state budget. This dispropor-tion between labor and value was definitive for petrostates. In the age of oil, there were countries like Qatar, economic powerhouses whose small populations were complemented by imported and unprotected labor. Their masters were as rich as sultans, which some of them were. There were countries like the US, which also traded fossil fuels and polluted the planet, but whose extracted energy was mostly used domesti-cally. There were also countries like Norway, which sold its oil but did not spend the profits, polluting the planet but refusing to corrupt itself. And finally, there were populous petrostates such as Russia, Venezuela and Iran.

For these petrostates, oil and gas played the role of the almighty resources featured in twenty-first-century movies – unobtainium in *Avatar*, spice in *Dune*, or even the ring in *The Lord of the Rings*. Based on fictions created in paleomodernity, these films mocked that era's archaic resource-dependency for the young gaiamodern public. The obsession with oil was typi-cal of the Western consumer. Petrostates were addicted not so much to oil as to money. Relying on their single-product export, they saw it as the all-powerful solution to their mul-tiple problems. It was export – with all its connected issues of transportation, financialization and securitization – rather than extraction that defined the petrostate. OPEC, the world-wide cartel of petrostates, meant an organization of petroleum *exporting* countries; an organization of petroleum *extracting* countries would have been a very different mix.

For those in the business of exploiting natural resources, transportation costs can exceed extraction costs by order of magnitude. The oil-extracting regions of Western Siberia, for example, were separated from Russia's industrial centers and from Western consumers by thousands of miles. Characteristic of Russia's type of colonization, these internal distances amplified intra-country inequalities. Since oil extraction did not require much labor, the wealth it generated did not accrue to the Russian people. The state spent or saved the profits, leaving the population to rely on subsistence incomes.

Norway and the United States were not petrostates, but Russia and Venezuela were. While these latter two countries were vastly different, both combined oil with authoritarianism, using socialism to deceive their peoples and proceeds from the oil trade to feed them. Devastated by the oil curse and misman-agement, socialist Venezuela slid into chaos. The Soviet Union, a country created by a party of the utopian left, turned into the far-right Putinist Russia.

Connecting two political realities, the Russian state and oil, Harvard scholar Marshall Goldman dubbed Russia a petrostate in 2008.[4] The meaning of this concept shifted from the sultanates to those countries that had both oil *and* a large population. They were clearly divided into two groups: some exported most of their oil, others burned it domestically. Exporting petrostates functioned like the old mercantilist empires: more barrels per capita meant a higher income for the state, while the people remained poor. In contrast, those countries that extracted but did not export their oil secured their growth by boosting con-sumption domestically. Like the United States and Australia, Russia had a large population, but in exporting most of its energy it used oil and gas revenues in the same way as Saudi

Arabia or Qatar. It was not the amount of carbon extracted but the country's dependence on oil exports that turned it into a petrostate. The oil curse played a particularly vicious role in Russian domestic affairs precisely because it had a large and well-educated population that benefited little from the oil and gas revenues (see Chapter 6). In the early 1990s, neoliberal economists from Harvard described Russia as an Upper Volta with rockets. In fact, it was more like a Qatar with people.

As long as capitalism has existed, monopoly has been its highest manifestation and worst nemesis. Every petrostate was a *double monopoly*, because each combined a monopoly on violence with a monopoly on energy. The former was a traditional attribute of the state; the latter emerged through the nationalization of oil production after World War II, and in Russia through the consolidation of Putin's power in the early 2000s. With OPEC+ (where the plus sign stands for Russia), a *triple monopoly* emerged: controlling 55 percent of global output and almost all proven reserves, this expanded cartel had the power to set global prices. But no monopoly is perfect. Thankfully for the world, the members of this cartel had opposing interests and allegiances, differences that Russia's war on Ukraine only exacerbated.[5]

Every economist knows that if the products of labor are monopolized then their quality will decrease and their price increase. Whether we're talking about Mercedes and BMW, Microsoft and Apple or Harvard and Yale, we do not allow them to merge because we think that competition improves their outputs. However, we do not apply this belief to primary commodities, and twentieth-century states were happy to see them monopolized. This happened because raw materials were not the products of labor. Extraction did not fit the seemingly universal laws that political economy had formulated for production.

In extraction, there was no economy of scale: if you enlarge your shoe or car factory every unit will be cheaper, but if you expand your corn or oil field every unit will be more expensive (classical economists called it the law of diminishing returns). There was no relation between extraction costs and exchange value. There was no connection between productivity and human capital or property rights – these were critical for production but neutral for extraction. Finally, there was no relation between taxation and representation: the main income of resource-bound countries came from customs duties and royalties rather than from taxes. The deepest foundation of modern economics, the labor theory of value, did not work in the resource-bound states. It was a whim of nature rather than human labor that made these states, and their leaders, richer or poorer.

Your curse is someone else's blessing

Different natural resources have different political features, or, as Bruno Latour put it, tell different stories.[6] Political scientist Michael Ross enumerated four features of oil rent:[7] It was *large*, so the governments of petrostates were twice as big as that of their neighbors. It was *direct*, so treasuries depended on the state-owned oil fields rather than on taxes. It was *unstable*, because global oil prices were beyond the control of any single state. Coming from nature and bypassing people, it was *opaque*. These features made oil rent an optimal means for enriching a state-sponsored elite. Since its main source of income, oil extraction, was not labor intensive, the petrostate did not depend on its population. Hiding its fabulous wealth, the petrostate produced lofty promises and embarked on military adventures. The early twenty-first-century statistics showed that a country's export of oil and gas hindered its democratic development, destroyed other sources of national income, and depressed human capital. Economic growth in the exporting petrostates went hand in hand with the incompetence of the ruling elite, who consolidated their power in order to amass even more wealth.

Imagine two states that trade with one another. Their relations could be beneficial for both insofar as they create new value together through trade and labor. But it also could be a zero-sum game, or these two states could destroy the value they had created. Let's take another step. Our two ideal-type countries are as different as they could be: one relies almost entirely on natural resources, the other on the labor of its people. Both have comparative advantages which develop and sharpen while they are trading (for proving this point, Paul Krugman was awarded the Nobel Prize in economics[8]). Now, the labor-dependent state acts as it should according to Adam Smith or Paul Krugman: it protects property rights, breaks monopolies, encourages technical progress, delivers education to its citizens, provides public services and collects taxes. This state has a robust economy, a brimming treasury and a happy people.

With the resource-dependent state things are different. It owns a rare and valuable natural resource – say, sugar cane, diamonds, oil or rare metals. Possessed of such treasure, this state must protect it from rivals and secure the long lines of transportation to its consumers. Its resource is expensive precisely because it is rare, difficult to reach and risky to protect. Maximum profits can be achieved through the formation of a monopoly, or maybe a cartel, which has the pricing power and is allied to powerful state agencies. Only a combination of rising prices, decreasing risks and increasing sales will secure the desired growth.

The loop goes through the state, which lends the extractive monopoly its protective power. An *oiligarch* either cheats, bribes or buys out the state. If he is a Rockefeller he underprices his rivals and acquires their oil fields, creating a monopoly which leaves only the state as his rival; at this point, he either wins or loses, and even if he loses he may win again later. But if he is a Putin he starts from the opposite end: using the power of the state, he confiscates one field after another and coalesces them into a monopoly that takes on the appearance of having become the state itself. Historically, this top-down strategy proved to be the more successful. You trade a resource which is central to the state, and the state provides you with all its power to secure your trade. Is it not only fair that you become the state?

The monopolistic rulers of resource-bound states do not guarantee property rights. They cannot rely on their own capital, keep it in the country or hand it down to their children. Along with their subjects, the rulers also suffer from the absence of public goods such as fair justice or clean air. Oiligarchs build their yachts with foreign firms and sail them in foreign seas, which are safer and cleaner. They prefer to settle their conflicts in foreign courts. Their spouses require private goods which only labor-dependent states are capable of offering. Their children need the kind of quality education that is only available beyond the border. If their currency is convertible, then textiles, gadgets and even weapons can be purchased abroad. But safe parks, clean beaches and good schools are not available for import. The middle class, always fragile in resource-bound states, also transfers its modest needs and pleasures beyond the border. This is the underlying cause of capital flight, in which people from resource-dependent states transfer their assets to labor-dependent states.

What is a resource curse for the extracting country is a blessing for its trade partners. Exported capital – a converted form of grain, timber, oil or gas – turns into a bank deposit in Switzerland, a chateau in France, a business venture in Germany or shares in American corporations. This capital, significant by any standards, brings profits to its recipients. The Swiss bank gets a percentage, London property prices skyrocket, and new businesses pay taxes in the host countries. If this wealth trickles down, then those who benefit live far away from the places where it was pumped or mined. Paradoxically, the resource-holding elite invests in the same institutions abroad that it neglects, or even destroys, at home: the legal system, universities, parks and hospitals. According to John Rawls's principles of justice, it is morally right if some people become richer than others as long as the poorest do better as a result.[9] In resource-dependent economies, the first possibility is realized in one place while the second is realized in another. Wealth trickles down far away from the places where it has been created. Disparities are doomed to grow.

Loss of industry

After 1991, neoliberal reforms left millions of Russians on the brink of survival. Among the victims were the Soviet-era intelligentsia – scientists, engineers and other professionals whose careers were previously guaranteed by the state and protected from international competition. Deindustrialization hollowed out the big Russian cities that had sprung up around paleo-modern factories, mining agglomerations and military plants. But unemployment remained relatively low. By subsidizing coal and gas for industry, and diesel fuel for farms, the government supported the circulation of goods and food throughout the country. It was a special kind of sustainability, secured by traditionally low salaries, gradual depopulation and fossil fuel subsidies. All this made the deindustrialization process even more dramatic. Received in exchange for carbon, hi-tech imports displaced locally manufactured goods. The mining and steel-making agglomerations of the Urals and Siberia were so dependent on military procurements that they could not survive the détente of the 1990s. The rate of return on oil and gas developments was higher than the risky profits from airplanes and nuclear reactors. The country lost most of its civil engineers and metal workers. In the 2010s, none of the machines needed to manufacture other machines were made in Russia. With the reduction in demand, the Soviet competences of long-term planning and reverse engineering were quickly lost.

With Putin's war in Ukraine and the resulting Western sanctions, all this became clearer than ever. The Russian military used foreign-made chips and sensors that were awkwardly installed in its Soviet-designed armor. A study of Russian weapons recovered in Ukraine in 2022 showed that they routinely used imported devices, which had been illegally smuggled from Western countries by state-owned manufacturers.[10] Alexander Kuleshov, the head of Skoltech University that was founded in 2011 in Moscow in collaboration with MIT, admitted that all its high-tech equipment was imported. Because of the sanctions, if a chip in his supercomputer stopped working, he would have to spend months organizing a replacement shipment from Europe. In the 1980s, Kuleshov explained, Soviet engineers would take an American processor and abrade it, reengineering the chip layer by layer. This worked up until the launch of the 386 processor, created by Intel in 1986. Subsequent processors were so thin that they couldn't abrade them. Since then, no chips have been produced in Russia.[11] Sanctions made it impossible to import them and difficult to substitute them: in order to make one chip, you need many others, and how could you make a chip if you couldn't get your hands on any?

Cars were an element of paleomodernity that survived into the new era. From the 1960s, global standards required that motor vehicles have safety belts and lights; later, airbags were made mandatory. A new revolution in the auto industry started together with the revolution that buried the Soviet Union. In 1992, the Euro 1 directive stipulated the maximum emissions for all cars sold in Europe. Russia adopted this standard in 1997; until recently, it was not possible to register a car in Russia that was inferior to the Euro 5 standard. Safety belts belong to paleomodernity, emission standards to gaiamodernity, but they should work together in every car. Better, cheaper cars complying to the standards were assembled in Russia from ready-made foreign parts. The old Soviet car factories were shut and repurposed. For German or American corporations, it was cheaper to build an assembly factory from scratch than to reconstruct an old Soviet shell. The poor, however, still drove old cars that did not meet modern standards, and Russia had the highest number of road deaths per population in the world.[12] In response to the invasion of Ukraine, the major car corporations left Russia. Having appropriated their assembly lines, native businesses could not make cars that met the EU standards. The solution was simple: in April 2022, the government issued a decree that abolished the European requirements for Russian-made cars. Free to pollute, they were no longer fitted with airbags.

Even in the mundane sector of construction materials, Russia's industrial dependence was total. The construction industry preferred local components: bulky and inexpensive, they were produced in proximity to the construction sites. However, in June 2022, it became clear that even the fabrication of these components – from bricks to pigments to nails – required imported materials. The factories hoped to source replacements from China and Iran, and spoke of "the barbarization of production."[13]

With two-thirds of its territory having no access to the grid, the country needed alternative sources of energy. As a producer of hydropower, Russia ranked seventh in the world, competing with Japan and Norway. In nuclear energy, another relic of paleomodernity that survived into the new era, Russia was a major player. But progress in the use of renewables such as solar and wind was painfully slow. Even with their prices plummeting, renewable energy was still more costly than burning domestic gas or coal. Although the government was awash with money and could buy any number of solar panels or wind turbines, it chose not to. In 2010, at a business conference in Berlin, Putin mocked the very idea of an energy transition.

"I do not understand what fuel you will use for heating. You do not want gas, you are not developing the nuclear power industry, so you will make heat from firewood?" Putin asked the audience. "You will have to go to Siberia to buy the firewood there."[14] Ten years later, solar and wind together made up less than 0.5 percent of Russia's energy production, compared to 42 percent in Germany and 10 percent in China. Per capita, Russia produced six watts of wind energy a year, compared to 1,000 in Denmark and 200 in China.[15]

In 2007, the government created the Russian Corporation of Nanotechnologies (Rusnano), entrusted with the development of chips, renewables and much else. One of the largest corporations in the country, Rusnano was led by Anatoly Chubais, a former head of the Russian Presidential Administration. The corporation had an enormous and non-transparent budget. From time to time, it leaked stories about its plans for natively produced laptops or solar panels, but such products never reached the market. From 2016, the corporation was on the edge of bankruptcy. In 2021, Chubais left Rusnano to become Putin's Representative for Sustainable Development. Even his startling confidence, however, was of little benefit in developing sustainability. In March 2022, as the Russian troops were approaching Kyiv, Chubais fled the country; reportedly, he was poisoned in August but survived.

When Russia launched its all-out war, the Europeans said goodbye to Russian oil, Putin's officials to their yachts, and Moscow hipsters to their smoothies. Rather than proving that Europe could not do without Russian energy, the war demonstrated the dependence of Russian industries on Western imports. Amazingly, even the printing of rubles required Swiss pigment, and the salmon on fish farms needed Norwegian food. With the advent of the war, neither rubles nor salmon looked the same.

The rubble and the ruble

Socialism was born in the era of coal. Fed by proletarian discipline, the new creed reflected and later shaped the life of large working collectives.[16] Coal mines and coal-powered industries were the cradle of social democracy. Social welfare states – Weimar Germany, New Deal America, the Britain of the Old Left – did not survive the era of oil. Eventually they turned to neoliberalism – the liquid modernity of flowing oil, floating prices and fleeing capitals.

From its beginnings, Soviet-style socialism depended on coal but dreamed of oil. At the start of the twentieth century, the oil boom in Baku, a distant colony on the Caspian Sea, enabled the Russian Empire to overtake its rivals in oil exports. Future Bolshevik leaders, including Stalin, Beria, Vyshinsky, and many others, got their revolutionary initiation on the oil fields of Baku. But the masses of organized workers – miners, dockers, railmen, steelmakers and smiths – toiled with labor-intensive coal. Organized in trade unions, they launched waves of industrial action such as the all-Russian October strike of 1905, which paralyzed the country. Trained in Baku, the future Soviet leaders preferred oil, which brought power and money with less work and less workers.[17]

During World War II, the oil-rich Caucasus was one of the main targets of the Nazi assault. Baku was not occupied but many drills had been shut by the retreating Soviet troops. The American land-lease scheme supplied enough petrol and kerosine to the Soviets to win the war. The fields of Baku were depleting anyway. In the postwar period, Soviet geologists discovered abundant oil reserves in Tatarstan and later in Western Siberia; Stalin and Brezhnev affectionately called these new sources of revenue the Second and Third Bakus. Siberian oil was a boon for the Soviet leaders, granting them a decade of stability.

Oil exports secured the Soviet Union's state capacity and enabled its military build-up. In the late 1970s, new pipelines delivered oil and gas from Western Siberia to Western Europe. However, their crucial elements were manufactured in Germany or the US. Exchanging native oil for foreign grain compensated for the astounding inability of the Soviet system to produce food for its citizens (before and after the Soviets, Russia was a major exporter of grain). North American wheat fed the Soviet cattle which fed the Russian people. But soon it became clear that it would be cheaper to buy frozen meat abroad, and the cattle disappeared. Fresh into power in 1985, Mikhail Gorbachev was very much concerned about the depleting oil reserves: the entire country depended on them for sustenance. The drop in oil prices plunged the Soviet budget into a deficit that billions in foreign aid couldn't fix. It fell upon Boris Yeltsin's government to carry out its economic reforms at a time of cheap oil. In 2000, when Yeltsin appointed Putin to be his successor, oil prices rose again. The Fat Years of oil-fed prosperity began, and the renewed propaganda machine attributed this success to the young president.

The new rulers of Russia discovered that Western knowledge could resolve all issues of oil extraction and transportation in exchange for a fraction of the exported treasure. Not only could grain and meat be bought this way, but also car factories, pipelines and managers. Between 1999 and 2004, the output of Russian oil fields increased by 50 percent. Global prices were also rising, and the Siberian exports almost doubled in cash value. But these were only the direct receipts from foreign trade; a portion of the extracted fuel was consumed within the country at subsidized prices, bringing taxes to the treasury and amplifying state profits through the "funnel effect."[18] Taking this into account, we see about half of Russian GDP created by fossil fuels. The exchange value of the ruble obediently followed the price of oil. The physicist Boris Nemtsov, a leader of the anti-Putin opposition who was murdered in 2015, proposed a linear formula for the relation between the value of a ruble and the price of a barrel of oil: in dollars, these two curves floated as one. The efforts of millions of Russian workers, farmers and intellectuals had no impact on the price of the ruble. The entire Russian economy relied on the oil fields of Western Siberia.

The burning of gas, oil and coal for domestic needs diverted a valuable resource from the foreign market and decreased the revenue of the state. This was a burden the government sought to reduce. "Checking consumption in the mother country," as they put it in the nineteenth century, was a traditional task of the mercantile empires: the less people consumed domestically, the more would go to the treasury. The small Gulf-style petrostates relied on underpaid migrant workers for labor. But sustaining extreme levels of inequality was more difficult for petrostates with large native populations, such as Russia, Nigeria, Indonesia, Venezuela and, until recently, Mexico. Their carbon incomes were sufficient for meeting the demands of the elite, but never enough for supporting the people. Balancing these tasks was easier in times of growth and more difficult during slumps, when these governments regularly announced plans for diversification and modernization. None of these promises were ever kept.

Only a religious or nationalist narrative could explain the fateful chance that endows some countries with an abundance of resources and others with none. God or chance arranged things so that the distribution of oil largely maps onto confessional divides. In the 2000s, Islamic countries exported more than half of global oil.[19] There was also a link with an ideology, even if one now mostly abandoned: a quarter of global oil was extracted in three post-socialist countries – Russia, Venezuela and Kazakhstan. Eager to understand the meaning of their blessing, the oil-rich elites reworked the idea of a chosen people. Mystical nationalism helped them to distinguish between their own peoples, who received the state's charity, and aliens who did not. For the elite, charity confirmed their self-awareness as a chosen people who had earned their wealth and spent it wisely. For the population, this narrative turned citizens into paupers, working people into beggars. Ideal for corruption, fossilized carbon proved to be an unreliable foundation for a state. It became part of a vicious circle of evil that led to aggression outside and degeneration inside these countries.

Monopolizing the oil and gas trade, the state separated petro-revenues from the economic life of the country. Critically analyzed by the early British economists, the experience of the mercantilist empires provided a playbook for further action: raise exports, restrain internal consumption, keep the trade balance positive, accumulate gold in the treasury and invest in colonial expansion. Between 2009 and 2019, the amount of gold in the Russian treasury increased threefold while the economy grew only by a quarter.[20] The education budget was falling, the pension deficit was rising, and capital was fleeing the country. The gold reserves increased at unbelievable speed, competing only with military expenditures. Britain had seven times less gold, although its economy was larger than Russia's. The population of India possessed more personal gold than any other country, but the Indian state had three times less gold than Russia. And even China, whose economy was many times larger than Russia's, had less gold. Russia's reserves were huge, but gold did not save Putin from himself.

Norway had proven that an oil-exporting country could be peaceful and prosperous, but with a caveat. The Norwegian way consisted in locking oil and gas incomes into a special fund and forgetting about them, while developing alternative, counter-cyclical sources of revenue. In 2004, following the Norwegian model, Aleksey Kudrin created the Russian Stabilization Fund. It accumulated petrodollars according to the "budget rule." Annually, the government defined a certain price level, the so-called "cutting price." When the global price exceeded this level, the government transferred the surplus to the Stabilization Fund, which then invested in American and global securities. Close to Putin, Kudrin served as minister of finance but lost his post in 2011 because of his refusal to increase military expenditure during the "modernizing" presidency of Dmitry Medvedev. Ironically, Kudrin became the Chairman of the Accounts Chamber, the top financial control agency. An economist with the airs of a professor, Kudrin also found time to create modern educational facilities. However, acting as top auditor at a time of nationwide graft proved to be quite a challenge. His Stabilization Fund used fashionable terms such as "sterilization" but it lacked stability – and sterility too. The problem was that while the Russian people, just like the Norwegians, could probably have survived without oil, the Russian state could not. Having peaked in 2008, the Fund was restructured several times – no institution in the Russian Federation was renamed so often. By 2017, the Fund had lost a half of its assets, and in 2022 most of the money remaining in it was seized by sanctions.

The project of turning Russia into a bigger Norway failed. But Norway also had serious issues. Why did the Norwegians pump oil at all? Good for them that they did not use the profits, but would it not have been better for all if they'd left the oil and gas in the depths where they belonged? Financial engineering was no better fitted to resolving the problems of the Anthropocene than geoengineering. The German economist Felix Creutzig suggested measures that would reduce Europe's dependence on Russian energy by half every year, and would also reduce global emissions by 3 percent a year. Three sectors would be central – transport, building and food. Europeans would have to drive and fly less, switch to teleconferencing instead of commuting, reduce speed limits, turn down the heating in winter and the air-conditioning in summer, eat less meat, subsidize public transport and boost social equality.[21] These policies would have resulted in negative growth. But would not it be easier to experience degrowth than to live through war? Small is beautiful, cheap is enjoyable, and the best things that people do require less energy than the worst.

3

Parasitic Governance

A balance between the state and civil society – the condition for inclusive progress – is possible only if the state depends on the labor of its people. The founders of political economy believed this would be always true, but it is not. If the state owns natural sources of wealth and society does not have access to those sources, no equilibrium between them is feasible. In an extractive economy, the state turns into a trader of raw materials. Bureaucracy redistributes the wealth drawn from the depths of the earth, reserving a generous helping for itself. Competence being irrelevant, the bureaucracy turns into an "elite" – a close circle of people characterized by mutual enrichment, embedded loyalty and hostility towards outsiders.

The parasitic state is a political community that maintains the attributes of a state but fails to fulfil its functions. Instead of the old imperial 'progress' we see the triumph of archaic beliefs, demodernization and decay. Instead of being a source of national wealth, the people become recipients of state charity. Health services and education are irrelevant for the national economy. The population becomes superfluous, as Hannah Arendt observed.[1] It wastes away not because of deliberate extermination but due to neglect and despair (see Chapter 6).

Imitating democratic politics and the market economy,[2] the parasitic state accumulates gold, limits internal consumption, pursues domestic oppression and, sooner or later, launches a war of aggression. Money, knowledge and people flee the country. The state is caught in a vicious circle: the more it relies on natural resources, the less it invests in human capital; the lower the human capital, the more parasitic is the state and the higher its dependence on resource extraction.

Enter privatization

Russia's first answer to its inherited Soviet troubles was privatization. What had belonged to the state should go to individual citizens. Preaching and practicing privatization, Putin described it in the following words: "Give the property away to whoever wants it. In two or three years it will end up in the right hands . . . of the effective owner."[3] But this libertarian dream would only be realized if competition was fair, property rights were secured by independent courts and the monetary system was in working order. All of these conditions were absent in post-Soviet Russia. Still, privatization worked well for the millions of Russians who lived in state-owned apartments: with a piece of paperwork, they became owners of a property that could be sold or rented. Apartments grew in value without changing hands, so the process worked very differently from that outlined in Putin's sermon. While the privatization of housing did create something like a middle class, it did so only in major cities, thereby boosting geographical inequality rather than reducing it.

A parallel scheme was the voucher campaign. Launched by Anatoly Chubais, the vouchers were special securities distributed by the government to every Russian citizen for investment in a chosen company.[4] It was a bureaucratic success, but people soon found that their vouchers were showing miserable returns. Commoners compared Chubais's vouchers to Stalin's bonds, which could only be used as wallpaper. "What did you do with your voucher?," journalists once asked Putin. "I lost it," he responded.[5] Running out of money, the government launched a "loan-for-shares" scheme, which gave oil fields, potash mines, steel-making factories and much else to private creditors.

Western experts had drawn up respectable blueprints for privatization. A group of Harvard Boys – high-profile academics with close ties to the Clinton administration, such as Lawrence Summers, Jeffrey Sachs and Andrei Shleifer – played a role in Russia similar to that played in Chile by the Chicago Boys, the economists who had advised the Pinochet dictatorship. Years later, Sachs reflected: "People told me how incredibly crooked the whole thing was. It seemed pretty distasteful to me. I didn't like it."[6] The Russian-born Shleifer advised the Kremlin from 1992 to 1997. His Harvard mentor, Summers, was then serving as Under Secretary of the Treasury. Together, they managed the hundreds of millions that the US sent as financial aid to the Russian government, and wrote drafts of the new legislation.

Half a century earlier, Trotsky had warned that turning directors into owners would be a mistake: the bureaucrats would be happy but no progress would come out of it.[7] It so happened that Trotsky was correct and Summers wrong. Delayed salary payments, redundancies and murders dominated the news. In 2004, Paul Khlebnikov, a Russian-American journalist, was killed in Moscow while reporting on corruption for *Forbes*; he was one of the first victims of Russia's war against muckraking journalists. It also turned out that Andrei Shleifer had been investing in Russian securities in violation of conflict-of-interest rules. The US government sued Harvard University. The case was settled in 2005; both the University and Shleifer paid out millions of dollars in fines – it was the biggest settlement in Harvard's history.[8] Summers became the President of Harvard but resigned following another scandal in 2006. Known for his math-heavy publications, Shleifer remained at Harvard.

By privatizing agricultural land, the Kremlin transformed the old Soviet collective farms into agricultural corporations. Rural workers were retained on salaries; despite privatization they did not own their land or tools. Still, the production of grain and other staples increased significantly, and the country became a major exporter of food. Big agricultural holdings, some of them as large as European states, produced staple crops such as wheat, sunflower seeds and sugar beets. Oligarchs bought yachts and villas with the profits, but agriculture's share of GDP was decreasing every year. Export of grain was growing, but oil and gas accounted for more than 90 percent of the annual profits of Russian businesses. The new oligarchs hedged their assets by buying land. One example is Vladimir Evtushenkov, who began by purchasing a majority stake in the privatized Moscow Telephone Network. In 2009, he bought oil and gas fields in Bashkiria and an agricultural holding near Moscow. In 2014, he was charged with money laundering – the most powerful oilman in Russia, Igor Sechin, wanted his assets. Three years later, Putin passed the Bashkirian oil fields to Sechin, but left Evtushenkov the non-oil parts of his estate. In 2018, Dmitry Patrushev, a son of the director of Russia's security service (FSB), became the minister of agriculture. The young Patrushev was a member of the board of Gazprom and had a PhD in economics. It was proven that he had massively plagiarized his dissertation.

Members of the Soviet collective farms had used (but did not own) micro-slots of land, mostly vegetable gardens. After 1991, millions of peasants and dacha owners privatized their small households and gardens. In 1999, a quarter of the Russian population owned a subsidiary plot and was cultivating it. They worked 7 percent of the country's arable land but produced more than 40 percent of its agricultural output. Amazingly, they provided 92 percent of Russia's potato harvest, three quarters of its vegetables, almost all of its fruit, and half of its milk and meat.[9] In 2009, the numbers were similar.[10] This was an intensive but premodern agribusiness: whole families worked with shovels on miniscule plots, while elderly women sat on the side of the road, selling herbs by the gram or potatoes by the kilo. But these people were free: the only levy they paid was property tax; they chose their seeds, tools and methods; they owned their land and could sell it whenever they so desired. Russian agriculture had the same two-tier structure as other sectors: one part of the system, populous but mostly poor, fed the ordinary folk with perishable produce that could not be exported; another part, small but wealthy, produced the staples at volume, selling them abroad for convertible cash.

Unlike the Soviet leaders, whose Marxist training and aversion to the West spurred them to reduce class differences, the leaders of the new Russia were instructed by top Harvard economists. They created the new rich whose yachts and villas grew bigger every year. When the Harvard Boys left, it turned out that the new Russian rich were just the same Soviet bureaucrats – lazy administrators on a flat learning curve. Competition and growth did emerge in those sectors of the economy that were close to final consumption, such as retail or restaurants. But while extractive industries and final services were booming, everything in the middle, the rest of the industrial economy, was collapsing. If there was growth, it followed the price of oil. You could be a good manager, a bad manager or an absentee manager, but this kind of growth would always be with you. Inequality grew frenetically. Economists from Harvard and Moscow alike believed that economic growth would be the source of all good in Russia, that accumulated wealth would trickle down to the poor, that the rising tide would lift all boats. In fact, it lifted only the yachts of the rich. The boats of the poor leaked, and they drowned in the tide.

Enter corruption

Rejecting Soviet institutions but preserving their cadres, Putinism developed a new, profoundly anti-socialist ability to appropriate wealth. But where did this wealth come from if Russia's institutions and businesses were generally so unproductive? The answer was old and Soviet: from trade in natural resources. Extraction, not production, was Putin's best hope and worst-kept secret. An enormous security apparatus and a corrupt bureaucracy recycled the wealth produced from holes in the earth rather than by the work of the people.

In the early 1990s, the Kremlin decided that while oil would be fully privatized, natural gas would remain in the hands of the state. Created in 1989, Gazprom was given control of Russia's gas sources, transportation infrastructure and trade. The former Soviet minister Viktor Chernomyrdin – a popular figure who combined grey-headed refinement with folkish sayings – was appointed chairman of Gazprom, before going on to become Russia's prime minister several years later. While the Russian government distributed oil fields to new owners in the name of competition, Chernomyrdin made sure that Gazprom remained the sole proprietor of Russian gas. In his words, this corporation, the largest in the country, was "a natural monopoly" and "the spine of Russia."[11] The reason was simple. To use an agricultural metaphor: while oil was like staple crops, natural gas was like potatoes in being equally difficult to store. Impossible to transport by sea without expensive liquefaction, gas remained an inland commodity.[12] Moved via a fixed network of pipelines or reserved in underground caverns, gas was sold on the basis of long-term, guaranteed contracts. Free markets preferred oil, but natural gas was ideal for a planned economy.

In 2003, the FSB arrested Mikhail Khodorkovsky, head of the Yukos oil company and the richest man in Russia. A product of the ill-fated privatization campaign, Yukos was not much different from other Russian oil companies in its exploitation of Soviet derricks, pipes and specialists. Drilling in the key fields of Western Siberia, it produced one-fifth of Russia's oil. Had a prospective merger with its rival Sibneft gone ahead, it would have become the fourth largest private company in the world. Unlike his rivals, Khodorkovsky was gradually Americanizing his company. Yukos had five Americans on its board and its chief financial officer was also American. In 2001, Khodorkovsky established the Open Russia Foundation, modelled after George Soros's Open Society. He also tried to reform Russian higher education, donating money to the Russian State University for Humanities in 2003 and appointing his deputy, Leonid Nevzlin, as its rector. That same year, at a televised meeting in the Kremlin, Khodorkovsky informed Putin that corruption was costing Russia thirty billion dollars a year, or 10–12 percent of GDP. He also spoke critically about Russian higher education: it was wrong to emphasize law and order over science and scholarship, he said. For Putin, both criticisms were shocking and their combination unprecedented. Khodorkovsky's arrest was followed by several trials and ten years in prison. From a business perspective, the timing was perfect for renationalizing his assets: the price of a barrel was rising steadily and would continue to do so for a number of years. The shining towers of the Kremlin were connected to the oily derricks of Western Siberia by elective affinities that passed through the forgotten towers of the Gulag.

The Yukos affair followed the capture of NTV, an independent television channel that had criticized the war in Chechnya and caricatured Putin. The NTV studio was stormed by police officers in 2001, and soon appropriated by the state-owned Gazprom. Nationalization of NTV and Yukos were the starting points of the long journey that culminated in Russia's annexation of Crimea, its meddling in the US elections and its war in Ukraine. By ordering political assassinations of whistleblowers such as Alexander Litvinenko (2006), Anna Politkovskaya

(2006), Sergey Magnitsky (2009) and Alexei Navalny (2020), the Kremlin only confirmed their shocking allegations. In the West, dozens of books were written about Russia's kleptocracy. But other schemes were too big to reveal. Though well-informed about what was happening in the country, the international community accepted even the most egregious manifestations of Putin's rule. Privatization was the mother of corruption; renationalization was its almighty, patriarchal father.

Led by Igor Sechin, the state-owned Rosneft company appropriated the Yukos oil fields. A linguist by training and a former KGB officer, Sechin had begun working with Putin in 1994. Aside from oil, he worked on a nuclear energy program for Venezuela, an arms deal with France, and negotiations with the Trump presidential campaign. While these projects failed, the renationalization of Russian oil was accomplished. Combining his formal control of the largest Russian oil company with his informal command of the FSB, Sechin personified the double monopoly of energy and violence that constituted the Russian state. Rosneft was the second-largest Russian company after Gazprom. The duality of oil and gas was mirrored in two rival structures, with Putin their indispensable arbiter.

In 2006, a new name appeared in this story: Sergei Tregub. A colonel in military intelligence, Tregub was tasked with reorganizing Yukos's assets. One of the most secretive Russian oiligarchs, he passed the Yukos oil fields in Siberia on to Rosneft. Alexei Navalny's team investigated Tregub in June 2022, while Navalny was in a high-security prison. Working for fifteen years as Putin's fixer, Tregub built neo-baroque palaces across the country, from the Black Sea to the Altai, using money embezzled from Gazprom and Rosneft. Operating through dozens of shell companies, Tregub and his people were the formal owners of Putin's properties. Tregub also owned shares in insurance companies and other businesses; his personal wealth was estimated at three billion dollars.[13]

In command of armed men who received their salaries from state agencies, he secured property rights for his bosses in the unstable environment they created for others.

Symbolically, Putin's most notorious crony, Evgeny Prigozhin, began his career as Putin's personal chef. Prigozhin organized supplies to the Russian military, a troll factory that churned out propaganda for Trump, and mercenary camps in Syria, Central Africa and Ukraine. Moving from kitchens at home to military camps abroad was quick and easy for people like Prigozhin. Failing to pay taxes, flouting regulations and possessing unlimited resources, these princes of darkness preached and practiced a turbo-charged Machiavellian politics with the sole purpose of spreading their corrupt influence. They had no fear of the state because they *were* the state. Inept managers, they were efficient corrupters.

In supplying Germany and other European countries with gas, Gazprom violated European rules by not allowing other suppliers to use its pipelines and reservoirs. Controlling about one-third of the continental market, it based its operations on long-term contracts, sometimes fixed for as long as twenty-five years. Several times, the European Commission questioned these practices and obliged Gazprom to follow the rules.[14] It decided that all long-term contracts should be terminated by 2049, which was still pretty-long term. In 2019, the European Parliament adopted binding legislation that required ownership of pipelines entering EU territory to be separated from ownership of the gas supply.[15] Again, Gazprom sabotaged the policy. It was only the consequences of the Russo-Ukrainian War that broke the fossilized spine of Russia.

Corruption, Masha Gessen wrote, was subservient to cruelty. "My biggest problem with Putin was not that he stole and amassed wealth; it was that he killed people, both by waging war and by fielding assassins."[16] The stolen wealth helped the corrupted state pay for its troops and assassins, but it also brought its own nemesis: because of corruption, no word in

Russia – no document, blueprint or spreadsheet – meant what it said. Unpunished and limitless, Russia's corruption boosted its cruelty but also hollowed it out: the weapons barely worked, the armor did not protect, inventions did not materialize, and soldiers despised their superiors. As the Ukrainian leaders realized early in the course of the war, Russian corruption was their best ally.

Combined with the liberalization of capital movement, free-floating corruption changed international relations. Increasingly liquid and flammable, this oil-like universe ceased to comply with Carl Schmitt's claim that distinguishing between friends and foes is essential for politics. This old-fashioned idea assumed that loyalties could not be bought, and that political actors were solid bodies rather than liquid flows. Watching how the Russian oiligarchs turned their foes into friends through a combination of carrots and sticks – bribes and blackmail – we leap from Schmitt's political universe to Navalny's. Polluting nature, carbon also corrupts humans: this double action is Gaia's revenge. Stolen wealth generates more evil per dollar than earned wealth. Every carbon-generated, tax-avoiding dollar has greater bribing and killing power than a labor-produced, regulated dollar. Seeking growth, corruption is imperialist in the same way as colonization was.

Enter conspiracy

The explosive growth of inequality led to prolific mythmaking: every national elite came up with its own fables to explain its privileged position among the populace.[17] Emotionally, the growing inequality provoked discontent, hatred and guilt. Behaviorally, it led to outright aggression. Cognitively, it led to conspiracy theories.

The memory of the Soviet collapse haunted the Russian rulers. Egor Gaidar, the mastermind of the Russian reforms, noted that falling oil prices had buried the Soviet Union.[18] It took only one interpretative step to move from Gaidar's scholarly theorizing to a form of magical thinking about the global plotters who were bent on destroying Russia. The higher the price of oil, the more aggressive were the words and deeds of the Russian authorities. Conversely, when the oil price fell, they mellowed.[19]

From hidden transcripts of the secretive elite, these fables turned into public displays that defined official policies.[20] Seeing the entire world as an enlarged Moscow, the elite fueled new cycles of demodernization. In 2008, the TV anchor Mikhail Leontyev argued that the financial crisis was an American plot against Russia. In a typical move from fantasy to officialdom, Leontyev was later appointed the spokesman and vice-president of Rosneft. In 2015, the FSB chief Nikolai Patrushev blamed the Obama administration for initiating the Ukrainian crisis. The Americans' objective, he claimed, was to capture Siberia's natural riches; this was known, Patrushev said, because the FSB could read the minds of US officials.[21] In 2019, Sergei Glazyev, Putin's economic advisor, alleged that President Zelensky was going to eliminate Russian-speakers in Ukraine and settle Israeli Jews there instead: this was the plan the Americans had laid out for the country.[22] Vladimir Yakunin, a former KGB officer and head of the Russian Railways corporation, stated that the global financial system was controlled from a glamorous room in a Manhattan skyscraper which he, Yakunin, had once visited. Anton Vaino, Putin's powerful chief of staff, believed in a mysterious device, the "nooscope," which controls interactions between people, the economy and nature. Tapping into global consciousness, the nooscope supposedly "detects and registers changes in the biosphere and in human activity."[23] Vaino's deputy, the former prime minister Sergei Kiriyenko, turned out to be an adept of "methodology," a Soviet method of behavior modification through "organizational games."[24] The hyperactive Kiriyenko later played a leading role in the war effort, reorganizing the occupied territories in the Donbas according to his "methodological" templates. His boss Vaino was largely invisible to the public. Nobody knew what he was doing: a nooscope made flesh.

Shaped by the servants of the petrostate, Russian conspiracy theories had to explain how oil prices were determined. Igor Sechin, the chief coordinator of the Russian fossil fuel trade, shared his views on the subject in September 2014. A barrel was then worth about $90, and Sechin asserted that the price would remain stable for decades. Ninety dollars was "a good price," according to Sechin – a price that he could "work with." A year later, a barrel cost $60; Sechin was still working with it, but predicted that by 2035 it would cost $170. By September 2016, the price had dropped to $47 and Sechin's Rosneft had to ask the government for subsidies. Putin weighed in, stating that $47 was a good price, but it could be better: "oil prices should be fair," he added. It was not clear what he meant by fairness; the average cost of extraction of Russian oil was about $2 a barrel at the time, or $6 including transportation costs.[25]

In 2008, Alexei Miller, Putin's former secretary who became the head of Gazprom, dismissed the idea that American shale could compete with Russian gas. Shale gas was like "foie gras for the market," he said; its production in the US was "a well-planned PR campaign." In 2013, Miller said that the American shale industry was "a bubble that does not produce any profit."[26] But Miller's own corporation was on the brink of bankruptcy. All in all, Gazprom invested $320 billion in new drills and pipes, but most of them remained unused. The scandalous Nord Stream II, connecting Russia to Germany by circumventing Ukraine, cost Gazprom $15 billion. Never used, it mysteriously exploded in September 2022, along with its older sibling, Nord Stream I. But even during the war, Russian gas was flowing through Ukraine, and Gazprom was paying for its transit.

These pipelines could be the biggest machines humans have ever built. Will they eventually be used in the opposite direction, sending goods from Western Europe to Russia? A pneumatic mail system could make use of these pipes if Russian consumers were able to afford the deliveries.

Enter sanctions

The war led to sanctions, which led to the seizing of property, which in turn helped us all to discover many things that the Kremlin and its oiligarchs would rather have kept hidden. And yet much of it was already known. Mikhail Khodorkovsky had warned about the massive corruption in Russia right before his arrest in 2003. Alexei Navalny, before his arrest in 2021, guided us through the posh palaces of the Russian "elite." And the banks preferred by this elite – Credit Suisse, Deutsche Bank and a few others – also knew everything.

Transparency International found that in the years from 2008 to 2020, current and former Russian officials acquired 28,000 properties in eighty-five countries.[27] Dmitry Medvedev, one-time president of Russia and former head of Gazprom, owned one of the biggest villas in Tuscany. Vladimir Soloviev, a leading propagandist of Russia's state-owned TV, owned four properties on Lake Como. Petr Aven, a former minister and the co-owner of Alfa Bank, owned a flat in London, an estate in Surrey, a chalet in the Swiss Alps, a villa in Sardinia and twenty-eight properties in Latvia.[28] In May 2022, *Forbes* published awesome pictures, with price tags, of 124 properties held by twenty-two sanctioned Russian oligarchs – about five mansions per person.[29] Estimates of the value of Russian assets in Switzerland ranged from a conservative $25 billion calculated by the Swiss National Bank to the more realistic $209 billion put forward by the Swiss Bankers Association.[30]

Yachts were even more conspicuous than villas. Sailing the high seas or parked in coastal marinas, they flaunted the abundant luxury of the Russian oiligarchs. Igor Sechin owned two yachts. In 2022, France seized them both; the bigger one, 135 meters long, was estimated to be worth $600 million. But Sechin's vessel was of course smaller and cheaper than the yacht suspected to be owned by Putin: seized in Italy, this *Scheherazade* was 140 meters long and estimated at $700 million. Both were built in Northern Germany, at the Lürssen yard which also built ocean-going corvettes for the German navy – two times shorter and three times cheaper than the Russian yachts. No coincidence that this yard announced it was downsizing in September 2021.[31] The Russian cruiser *Moskva*, sunk by a Ukrainian missile, was longer than *Scheherazade* but of roughly equal weight. *Moskva* had a crew of 510 men, most of whom died on April 14, 2022; *Scheherazade* required ninety-four at full crew. Berthed at pier, the monstrous vessel was manned by fifty-eight crew members, who were flown between Moscow and Milan to service it in shifts.[32] Several other Russian yachts were seized on both sides of the Atlantic. The richest of the oligarchs, Roman Abramovich, who made his money on Russian oil and spent it on British football, owned five yachts, with a collective value of more than a billion dollars.

Anyone who had made that much money in a couple of decades must have been very busy indeed. Why did they want a yacht or two – or five? For entertainment? Many of these yacht owners supported Putin's war. Why did they keep their properties abroad? Even if we accept that a private entrepreneur like Abramovich could legitimately make enough to pay for his yachts, how was it possible for a civil servant like Sechin to do the same?

There is a story about Easter Island in the Pacific, where a local tribe kept erecting enormous stone statues, called "moai," until they had cut down all the palm trees needed to roll the statues to their places. When the first Western ships landed on the island, they found dozens of these grand statues standing on the deserted island, along with some left unfinished in quarries. But the natives were dying out.[33] The unused and unusable yachts of the Russian oiligarchs were akin to these ill-fated moai.

4

The So-Called Elite

Sometime around the mid-twentieth century, the now ubiquitous word 'elite' began to replace the old-fashioned term
'nobility'. In Russia, seventy years of Soviet socialism created a
society that was more equal than Western societies, though not
truly egalitarian. In 1953, the year of Stalin's death, more than 5
percent of the adult Soviet population was in prison – as many
as among black males in the United States today.[1] On the other
side of the barbed wire, thousands of privileged people – administrators, academics and others – enjoyed material benefits in
addition to their salaries. However, these benefits could not be
traded or passed on to their heirs. The dachas of Soviet officials bear no comparison to the villas of the Russian oligarchs,
and even top bureaucrats did not have yachts or villas in the
Mediterranean. Income inequality rose after Stalin's death, but
in the 1970s it was still lower than in major Western countries.[2]

Inequality

Starting from this lowly position, post-Soviet Russia witnessed
the fastest rise in inequality that has ever been seen worldwide.

All petrostates were highly unequal. On top of that, Russia maintained a flat income tax and refused to introduce an inheritance tax. Both policies distinguished Russia from other developed countries. Almost no other modern country, not even the United States under Republican administrations, went as far as Russia in adopting these libertarian policies.[3]

The most common measure of inequality is the Gini coefficient. As calculated by the government in 2018, Russia's Gini was 0.411 – a high number that made the Russian Federation comparable in income inequality to the United States. But the official statistics underrepresented top earners and underestimated inequality.[4] Using taxation data, French economist Thomas Piketty calculated the Russian Gini at 0.545, placing Russia among the world's most unequal nations.[5] His data did not include untaxed incomes – offshore accounts, grey trade schemes and kickbacks. Channeling money from the poor to the powerful, corruption increased the inequality of incomes. "In the global game of tax evasion, Russia became a world leader," wrote Piketty.[6] Using its own sources, Credit Suisse estimated Russia's Gini in 2020 as being higher than those of the US and the UK, and among big countries second only to Brazil. However, in inequality of wealth (rather than income), Russia tops the world. According to Credit Suisse, in Russia in 2021, 58 percent of national wealth belonged to the top 1 percent, well above Brazil (49%), the US (35%) and the UK (21%).[7] Two-thirds of Russian millionaires resided in Moscow, which was an incredibly high concentration of wealth for one city – the figure for London was about one-third.[8] Regional inequalities within the Russian Federation were far higher than anywhere else in the world. The richest US state paid 4.5 times more taxes per capita than the poorest, and the richest German land 2.5 times more. In Russia, the taxes per capita paid by the oil-extracting Khanty-Mansi region exceeded those of the overpopulated Ingushetia, in the Caucasus, by a factor of 300.[9] In a big country, this concentration of wealth was shocking.

Russia's population exceeded Qatar's by a factor of fifty, but the number of people who gained from oil and gas revenues in Russia was probably smaller than the total population of Qatar.

The Russian 1 percent

Studying post-Soviet Russia, sociologists described its society as being composed of a number of "estates,"[10] drawing on an historical concept that belonged to the Russian Empire. By law, imperial society was divided up into unequal "estates," named after the French *états*. The Imperial Code of Law prescribed different rights and duties for the gentry, the clergy, the urbanites and the peasantry: some estates paid taxes, others did not; some served in the army, others did not; and only some estates could enter university. In force until 1861, this structure – different laws for different groups – was unfair but lawful.

In contrast to the old Imperial Code, the post-Soviet constitution of Russia proclaimed equality for everyone. Structural inequality in twenty-first-century Russia was unconstitutional. However, it was huge and growing. Put simply, there were the commoners and the elite, and they lived in different political economies. From Caucasian farmers to Siberian workers to St. Petersburg designers, commoners exchanged the products of their labor within the borders of the country. The elite took part in a different political economy, in which natural resources were exchanged for Western luxuries, services and weapons. The larger part of the population lived like Turks or Romanians, whose median incomes were similar to those of Russians; the smaller part lived like the Qataris or the Saudis. These segments of society barely noticed one another: the middle class that could have connected them turned out to be a missing link.

The Russian class "pyramid" was in fact shaped more like a pear, with an enormous and impoverished bottom, a narrow waist representing the middle class, and a tiny head consisting of a miniscule number of people with enormous quantities of money. In the developed OECD countries, the middle class comprised a majority (61 percent in 2019). In Russia, the middle class accounted for "somewhere between 15% and 40% depending on the methodology," but the studies leaned towards the lower estimate.[11] Poverty was overwhelming. In 2022, more than one-fifth of Russia's citizens lived on less than ten dollars a day, and twenty-one million of them on less than two dollars. Although the state redistributed money across regions, classes and generations, it was never enough. Redistribution works better in economies that depend on labor, knowledge and capital; if you own oil, it is easy to forget about social justice. From Rockefeller to the Koch brothers to Putin, examples are plentiful.

In Russia's mining and extraction industries, salaries equaled 184 percent of the average wage; in finance, 220 percent. In the education and public health sectors, by contrast, wages were only 71 and 80 percent of the average.[12] Spending and earning rubles, all these people took part in the national economy. The value of their rubles was supported by oil. But even without this source of external revenue, Russia's working people would have established some sort of economy. It was the Russian state that would have found itself with no money.

Before 2022, Russia had 83 billionaires (*Forbes*), and 269,000 millionaires (Credit Swisse). The real number of the rich and powerful in Russia was somewhere between these two figures – just a few tens of thousands. We know very little about them. Among other privileges, they were free to shun public attention in any form – to decline interview requests, avoid sociological polls and evade tax inspectors. The lion's share of industrial assets and farmland was given to Soviet-era managers and administrators – exactly those people who had brought the country to the point of collapse in 1991. The leadership saw this way of privatization as the way to civil peace and market competition. If the most sought-after assets in Russia had been auto-makers or chip producers, privatization might have improved the economy. But the most coveted properties were oil fields, gas pipelines and metal-makers. They were desired precisely because their products were not subject to competition within or outside the country. Global prices for oil and metals were booming. Petrodollars began flooding into Russia. Several decades of scarcity ended with the Fat Years, as the 2000s came to be known in popular memory. From this point onwards, the government was able to buy everything and anyone. The increasingly well-funded state-owned propaganda machine attributed the country's successes to its leadership and its failures to foreign forces.

Given all the reforms that took place after 1991, the overlap between the late Soviet and the post-Soviet cadres was stunning. In 2003, the number of military and security officers in the Russian elite was estimated at one-fourth. Playing with words, sociologists called this system a militocracy – a far cry from meritocracy, but the gruesome reality of Putin's Russia.[13] This elite was playing the same role in the Russian Federation that the nobility played in the Russian Empire: they formed the exclusive pool of candidates for top positions in all branches of power – executive and representative, military and civil, central and regional. Moreover, the new elite was almost as hereditary as the old nobility. In 2020, researchers found out that around two-thirds of the Russian bureaucracy had parents who had also worked in the bureaucracy. Thirty years after the collapse of the Soviet system, the descendants of the Soviet officials made up about 60 percent of Russia's ruling class.[14]

The new elite mixed insiders from the military-security complex with graduates in finance, law and linguistics. The Soviet Politburo consisted mostly of trained engineers, and the State Planning Committee was run for decades by an oilman, Nikolay Baybakov. In contrast, top executive positions in post-Soviet Russia were rarely held by industry experts. It was more common for a security officer, a lawyer or even a journalist to hold a top position in an oil corporation than for an oilman to make a career in the civil service. The post-Soviet elite consisted of generalists rather than professionals. Its icon was Igor Sechin, the head of Rosneft, who trained as a linguist and then worked in foreign intelligence. These people shunned specialized knowledge, technical skills and public performances. They were equally eager to lead an oil business, a megapolis or a military campaign.

Almost all members of the elite had their offices in Moscow and their homes around it. This wealthy, decadent and occasionally rebellious enclave was vastly different from the other regions of the country. Full of West European managers and Central Asian migrants, Moscow was to Russia what London was to the UK, or Hong Kong to China. While other regions viewed the capital with jealousy and distrust, the government explained that Moscow was the engine of growth, which was particularly incredible when there was no growth. Even during the war, Moscow protected its privileges. While recruitment was expanded in the poorest and distant areas of the country, conscription was declared in the capital only when defeat made it unavoidable. "The normal, peaceful rhythm of life in Moscow" will be protected by any means, declared the mayor of the Russian capital in the disastrous November of 2022.[15]

Flight and fate

In the thirty years following the collapse of the Soviet Union, Russia changed from being the champion of equality to a country with the highest concentration of capital. And yet most of this capital was not in Russia. Counted in dollars, Russia's export of natural resources massively exceeded its imports of goods and services, with an annual trade surplus averaging 10 percent over a period of 25 years.[16] The equivalent of 200 percent of Russia's annual GDP went missing – more than three trillion dollars. The tucked away financial assets amounted to more than the total financial assets legally owned by Russian households.[17] The value of the stolen property far exceeded that of the Norwegian Oil Fund, the biggest in the world, which in summer 2022 had $1.2 trillion in assets (see Chapter 2).

After 2014 the Kremlin banned foreign vacations for many groups of mid- and high-level officials – a policy that was applied first to the military, and then to law enforcement and major industries. Corruption initially helped to avoid these prohibitions, but the Covid-19 lockdowns and, eventually, European sanctions increased the isolation of the Russian elite. The old life of the 2000s, with vacations in Turkey or Egypt, skiing in the Alps or shopping tours to London, never returned for these people. Imagine a high-up official, corrupt but rational. He worked in Moscow and had a life there, but invested his surplus wealth abroad. He bought a villa in Italy or a chalet in France, and had a yacht built in Germany. He and his family wished to spend as much time as possible enjoying these amenities – it was nicer and safer there than in Moscow. He got a residence permit for his chosen country, or even bought citizenship through the programs that were available in the UK, Malta, Cyprus or Latvia. His children went to a private school not far from his second home. His time abroad was limited to weekends and vacations, but his family preferred to spend more time there. Unexpectedly, Putin's order forbade him to go abroad – it was the price of Crimea, he was told (he could not care less about Crimea). For him, capital flight entailed a geographic separation of public and private life, and massive family problems. The separation led to health issues such as alcoholism or depression. He could not leave his position in Moscow because he had to support his family abroad. Western sanctions only added to his anxieties: when would he ever see his children? New and riskier operations got him into further trouble, and his family would suffer too.

The sheer numbers indicate that this could well have been a common scenario. From anecdotal evidence we know that the divorce rate among Russian officials was extraordinary; many had secret second families or frequented dating sites. Oligarchs had more freedom, but there was a huge overlap between oligarchy and officialdom, which formed the basis for corruption. Many of the protagonists featured in Navalny's investigative reports played both roles, oligarchic and official, at different stages of life. Like corruption, capital flight was a systemic feature of the Russian state, one of its constituent mechanisms.

The war forced hundreds of thousands of Russians, most of them young and educated urbanites, to leave the country. Expecting military mobilization and violence at home, they flew to Georgia, Armenia, Turkey or Kazakhstan – the countries that did not require visas. Most of them found themselves in a desperate situation, with no job, no money and no welfare support. Only the Kremlin applauded this displacement of the country's young and productive subjects: the very same people who might take part in the acts of protest and resistance were removing themselves from the domestic scene. At this point, education, high culture and public life became mere nuisances for the Russian rulers. For this small but greedy group whose lifeblood came from the trade in oil and gas, the people were redundant, and educated people a threat. Students and intellectuals led the anti-Putin protest movement in Moscow in 2011–2012, as they did the democratic movement in Ukraine. Revolutions historically occur in the capitals, and this was true even in a vast country like Russia. Exacerbating the demographic problems, the massive migration during the war was a blessing for the Putinist state.

Growth and democracy

"Thou shalt love thy neighbor as thyself," but still you and your neighbor and the beggar on the corner are all different. What is the moral justification for inequality? One argument appeals to meritocracy. A good worker should live well, so that he'll work even harder. A good manager secures work and prosperity for many people, so he should receive a higher salary.[18] Another argument appeals to infrastructure. As the British economist John Maynard Keynes wrote, without a concentration of wealth, no investment in infrastructure would be possible. The railways would not have been built had capital been equally distributed.[19] But Russia's infrastructure was still notoriously bad despite its billionaires.

During the 2000s, Russia experienced a dramatic shift to the right, and in the 2010s to the far right. Andrei Illarionov advised the young Putin to read Ayn Rand; later, Orthodox priests played the role of libertarian advisors to the aging dictator.[20] Separating rich from poor, huge fences crossed Russian villages as well as many cities; in happier countries, you would never see fences as high.[21] The new elite rejected not only common property and progressive taxation but human rights and democratic procedures. Carl Schmitt's decisionism and anti-Atlantic geopolitics became incredibly popular amongst intellectuals who had started with Marx and later, albeit briefly, admired Popper.

In the aftermath of the Cold War, a revived "modernization theory" stated that various aspects of development such as industrialization, urbanization and education all combined in shaping modernity. As prosperity led to democracy and democracy to prosperity, growth of incomes would bring democratization to every country.[22] I guess that this would have happened in an end-of-history universe. In fact, the supposed correlation between growth and democracy was positive only for productive countries that received most of their income from labor rather than from natural resources. In extractive countries, the opposite was true: the higher their incomes, the less democratic was their political regime. Unearned money does not bring freedom.

Acknowledging the problem, the Polish-American political scientist Adam Przeworski came up with a weaker formula: a rich country could be either democratic or authoritarian, but if a country has been both rich and democratic, it would never regress to authoritarianism.[23] But once again, in relation to Russia, this did not work: precisely when it developed into a high-income country it turned to a full authoritarianism. In 2020, Daniel Treisman, an American specialist in Russian politics, restored the strong version of modernization theory. Earlier, in 2005, Treisman and Shleifer had declared that Russia was "a normal country" with middle incomes and a democratic politics. It had problems such as corruption and inequality, the coauthors stated, but with further growth these problems would dissipate.[24] Fifteen years later, Treisman omitted Russia from his tables that allegedly demonstrated a connection between growth and democracy.[25]

Petrostates such as Russia, Iran, Venezuela, Saudi Arabia and others provide powerful counter-examples to modernization theory. In these oil-fed countries, people have no part in creating wealth and the national income does not reach them. In the 1990s, Russia was a poor but democratic country. In the 2010s, it was a high-income but authoritarian country. In the 2020s, it lost an imperial war and reverted to totalitarianism. Unusual as it was, Russia attempted to impose its paleomodern practices on other countries by various means such as propaganda, election interference and military invasion.

Authoritarianism is not a major problem for gaiamodernity; imperialism is. If the worst comes to the worst, an authoritarian turn might seem a sensible way to confront the climate crisis.[26] But there is no excuse for imperialism, which is nothing but a barbaric method of destroying the planet. As Anthony Giddens wrote, "the history of oil is the history of imperialism, in one guise or another."[27] Russia needed no guises. A combination of unearned income from fossil fuels and unearned protection by nuclear weapons produced an untested and overconfident elite. Peace hid the failures of these people behind inflated growth figures and rigged ballot boxes. The war revealed their incompetence, arrogance and impotence.

5

The Public Sphere

Putin's rule destroyed many sectors of national life, but it was the public sphere, a domain of culture and debate in which Russia was strong and respected among nations, that suffered the most. Compared to the late Soviet period, political control in Putin's Russia was more flexible and probably more efficient. In the mass media, change of ownership determined the transformation of content. The TV channels and newspapers that had been privatized after 1991 were renationalized even before the state recaptured its oil fields. Media and oil – both were of strategic importance and their fates were intertwined: NTV, the major media company massacred in 2000, fell into the hands of Gazprom. The former owners of these media companies were pressed into emigration, comfortable for some but deadly for others.

Following the Soviet model, the Kremlin generously supported apolitical arts that required much technical training, such as classical music and ballet. But in a new development, wads of cash were also dished out to individual divas, conductors and impresarios. The glamorous lifestyles of these people stood in sharp contrast to the Soviet past: performing in Russia and abroad, they enjoyed the best of both worlds. No surprise that many of them were grateful and, as the war would show, remained loyal to their patrons in the Kremlin. Sharing a patriarchal aversion to diversity and change, they cultivated narcissism, conspiracy theories and homophobia.[1] With the crisis of the Anthropocene, such anti-modern formations, and even more extreme examples such as QAnon, appeared in many nations. However, their active promotion by the elite was unusual, and in a highly unequal country such support meant a lot.

Mass media

Throughout the 2000s, the Kremlin did not interfere in the arts, humanities or even the social sciences. They could develop without censorship, but also received no support from the state. Writers, artists and scholars struggled for survival, but they shared this fate with colleagues in many Western countries. At the same time, the authorities and private patrons supported books, exhibitions and gala events that promoted fake science and alternative history. With no articulated policy, it just so happened that most post-Soviet cultural outlets turned out to be anti-American, Eurosceptic and homophobic. Stopmodernism was encrypted into news channels, reality shows, sporting events and beauty contests.

Over two decades, the top administrator in the Russian public sphere was Vladislav Surkov. Symbolically, he started his career in Yukos's security and ended it as the chief but informal administrator – a sort of viceroy – of the occupied Donbas.[2] Half-Chechen and half-Russian, Surkov had a reputation for being effective even though his endeavors failed one after another. Trained as a theater director, he climbed the ladder of power faster than his peers from the secret services. While working in the Presidential Administration, Surkov published a novel, *Close to Zero*, that was judged to be the epitome of Russian postmodernism. The protagonist is a professional writer and socialite who takes part in bloodthirsty activities in the Caucasus while maintaining a sexy Muscovite lifestyle. He ends up being tortured and mutilated in an ordeal screened for the viewing pleasure of Moscow connoisseurs. In 2015, Surkov oversaw the preparations for the Minsk-2 agreement, signed by Putin and Merkel, amongst others. Using a term derived from the medieval Spaniards, Surkov identified the Russian aims in Ukraine as "a reconquest."[3] In 2016, an odd group of Russian hackers, spies and oligarchs helped Donald Trump's presidential campaign, achieving a major success with limited means. Having staged this special operation, Surkov became Putin's representative for negotiations with the Trump administration.

Surkov drew a sharp divide between newspapers that claimed a national reach and those that cultivated specific niches. The Kremlin controlled the nationwide newspapers, which often bore their old Soviet names, such as *Izvestia*. These media outlets were dependent on advertisement and their main sponsors were resource-trading corporations. In contrast, the niche papers articulated a broad range of political positions, from ultra-nationalist to liberal. Over time, most of these outlets moved online. In line with Putin's shift from authoritarianism to imperialism, their editors were declared "foreign agents" and effectively banned from doing business in Russia. Most of these editors emigrated in 2022, and their authors emigrated as well.

In contrast to the Soviet decades, big media in post-Soviet Russia had large sums of convertible money at its disposal. Instead of the slow, verbose style of Soviet broadcasting, the new TV producers turned to the speedy over-sexualized formats of their Western counterparts.[4] Coached by Silvio Berlusconi, Russia Today, Channel One and other TV outlets employed visual tropes and technical equipment that looked distinctly familiar.[5] Indeed, they produced some of the worst examples of a fully commodified, ultra-capitalist culture one could imagine. In the budget for 2020, the TV expenditure of the Russian state was estimated at 1.3 billion euros. The biggest beneficiary was Russia Today, which broadcasted megatons of aggressive propaganda in several European languages.[6] Anchors of TV channels purchased villas on Lake Como or flats in London. With their kids attending private European schools and their spouses undergoing expensive plastic surgery, these propagandists were proud of their cosmopolitan lifestyles. They nevertheless broadcasted anti-modern anger and parochial nationalism with endless verve and outlandish duplicity. The very same people you might meet over a weekend in a posh Mediterranean hotel spent their working days cursing "gay Europe" from their studios in dusty Moscow.

Internet

For a vast, underpopulated country with a notoriously poor transportation network and major disparities between its regions, the internet was a blessing. However, telecommuting developed slowly in Russia. Seeing electronic communications as a strategic asset, the government created Svyazinvest, the fixed-line monopoly, in 1994. In a loan-for-shares scheme, the government refused to accept a bid by George Soros. Later, Soros described his involvement in the Russian communication business as "the worst investment he's ever made."[7] Confessing that he had "a soft spot for Russian intellectuals," Soros, more than anybody else at the time, was pushing Russia to come to terms with modernity.[8] Thousands of young scholars, journalists and artists received their first experience of creative freedom and fair pay from Soros's charity, Open Society, which was investing millions of dollars in Russia. His failure with Svyazinvest foreshadowed his gradual retreat from the country.

Across the former Soviet space, Russian-speakers perceived the internet as a much-needed platform for horizontal communication. By 2022, internet penetration in Russia was estimated at 89 percent – a little lower than in the UK but higher than in Italy, Poland or China. Spending almost eight hours online every day (one hour more than the world average), Russians now had less time to watch TV. However, a poll conducted in 2019 showed that Russians still spent a whopping 3 hours and 40 minutes per day watching TV, about an hour more than the European average. Internet-based services such as taxi rides or food deliveries remained the preserve of major cities. But in the 2010s, there were few bureaucrats who didn't use email, few drivers who didn't use satellite navigation and few scholars who didn't use Wikipedia. At the same time, Russian hackers developed their skills and the pro-Kremlin players created "troll factories." Either paid by the state or simply to entertain themselves, anonymous hackers moved from stealing money to leaking sensitive information that could change the course of an election in a foreign country. Their less skillful peers jammed online communications with fake news or random comments.[9]

In 2014, Putin began calling the internet "the CIA project," and the government started its campaign of taming the virtual space; as usual, an imperial invasion coincided with the domestic oppression.[10] Some sites were banned, other were slowed down, and search machines were obliged to deliver results in a pre-approved order. Every Western platform was doubled by a Russian one. Having created their Google analogue, Yandex, Russian engineers developed a Facebook analogue, VKontakte, and a WhatsApp analogue, Telegram. The Kremlin demanded that these platforms keep personal data in Russia, and gave grants to some of them. With the invasion of Ukraine in 2022, the government banned Facebook and slowed down Twitter, depriving almost fifty million Russian users of information and entertainment. In response, about 20 percent of them switched to VPNs, which were also banned. However, the government failed to block VPN services, and they continued to work fine, connecting millions of Russians to the outside world.

As the biggest IT corporation in Russia, Yandex ran a news channel that before the war drew thirty million Russian users. During the war, its algorithms guided readers in such a way that searching Yandex News for the words "war" or "invasion" yielded no results. Whistleblowers reported this practice, and in March 2022 the EU sanctioned the company.[11] Telegram remained a highly popular social messenger app and news provider, but nobody knew how secure its encrypted data was. The Kremlin mooted the idea of banning Wikipedia and creating a Russian analogue that would provide historical information in a nationalist key. In 2021, sociologists noted a growing number of young people who used the internet and ignored TV, but about a half of Russians used both medias intermittently. With the launch of the invasion, the Kremlin's arbitrage between the well-controlled national television channels and the foreign-owned, privately used internet failed completely. Many Russian patriots, nationalists and stopmodernists maintained popular blogs on social media. But when the EU sanctioned Russia Today, YouTube, TikTok and Telegram kicked RT off their platforms in fear of new sanctions. It was a powerful sign that, despite close control by the Kremlin, media platforms were more afraid of global sanctions than of Moscow's bans.

Universities

Students, intellectuals and IT workers dominated Russia's protest movement of 2011–12 and Ukraine's democratic revolution. While they won in Ukraine, they lost in Russia, and this had enormous consequences. In Russia, the protesters manifested an overwhelming distrust of the state that had cheated them, but they were not angry enough to claim their rights.

British sociologist Samuel A. Green described this dynamic as "a retreat from the public space."[12] But, as we will see in the next chapter, the private sphere was barely able to give refuge to these people. The hope was for the new generation and their education.

In 2003, Russia joined the Bologna Process, which involved restructuring higher education programs according to European standards. But the international rankings of Russian universities failed to improve. In 2010, not a single Russian university made it into the top 200 in the *Times Higher Education* list. In 2012, the government launched "Project 5:100." The idea was to increase the global rankings of leading Russian universities by making professors' salaries dependent on their citation index. Despite considerable investment, this multi-year program was also a failure. In 2021, the Accounts Chamber – the chief auditor – concluded that not a single Russian university had made it into the top 100. In the meantime, the auditors and newspapers reported the salaries of the rectors, which were tens, and in some cases hundreds of times higher than those of the professors.[13] Led by such rectors, the established universities of Moscow and St. Petersburg exploited their prestige but produced inferior or even fake scholarship for decades. Newly established institutions were more successful. Some of them quickly grew to become some of the biggest universities in Europe, such as the Higher School of Economics (HSE), which became a major landowner in Moscow, and the Presidential Academy (RANEPA) with its fifty-five provincial branches.

Universities were not the only bastions of Russian science and scholarship. There was also the Academy of Sciences, a legacy institution left over from Soviet times. A gigantic non-profit organization, it included a thousand institutions in all fields of knowledge. A typical institution had hundreds of research associates, most of them with doctorates. These institutions were housed in some of the fanciest buildings in the major Russian cities. They did not have students, and education was not their function: they were involved in "research." At the top of these institutions were the "full academicians" who sat on the board of the Academy. In 2022, there were more than 300 such academicians, with an average age of seventy-six.[14] The whole system depended on the state budget, which was now shrinking. Many institutions generated extra income by letting their properties to businesses. This archaic system was barely subject to oversight by authorities or auditors, and the professors' salaries were pathetic. Many left the Academy's institutions for universities, while younger scientists emigrated.

Plagiarism was a particular issue in Russian academic life. Affecting many countries, it was widespread in Russia for cultural reasons. Coming from Soviet-educated families with their respect for high culture, the new Russian elite considered an academic degree an important addition to their status. Written by a ghostwriter, a dissertation could be bought cheaply. In 2016, Dissernet, an informal organization of scientists who hunted for cases of plagiarism, discovered that one in nine members of the Russian Parliament (Duma) had obtained academic degrees with plagiarized or ghostwritten theses. "A Russian Donald Trump would certainly have a PhD – maybe two or three," wrote one of the Dissernet leaders.[15] Plagiarism was identified in Vladimir Putin's PhD dissertation in economics, in a dissertation by Sergei Naryshkin, the chairman of the Duma, and in thousands of others. None of the well-heeled officials embroiled in the scandal resigned. Academic plagiarism was a form of corruption, more sophisticated but less convertible than the appropriation of rubles or barrels.

For similar reasons, attempts to create private institutions of higher learning were rarely successful. However, new independent universities were established in the sensitive areas of the social sciences and humanities: the European University at St. Petersburg, the New Economic School, the Moscow School of Social and Economic Sciences (Shaninka) and Smolny College, which remained a part of the St. Petersburg State University.

All these elite institutions were set up in the 1990s with the help of George Soros. All developed into modern hubs for the liberal arts and social sciences, securing foreign grants, attracting international professors, running joint programs with foreign schools and producing successful alumni who taught across the world. All had issues with the authorities, who tested out their growing anti-intellectual policies on these institutions.

The European University at St. Petersburg was closed twice, first in 2008 and again in 2017, but each time reopened following an intense struggle. The Rector of the New Economic School, Sergey Guriev, fled Russia for Paris in 2013 as a political émigré. The Rector of Shaninka, Sergei Zuev, and the Rector of RANEPA, Vladimir Mau, were arrested. Yaroslav Kuzminov, Rector of the gigantic HSE (and the husband of Elvira Nabiullina, head of the Russian Central Bank), resigned. The story of Smolny College, established in 1994 as a joint venture between the St. Petersburg State University and Bard College, New York, was unusual. Led by the powerful Aleksey Kudrin, the only heavyweight in Russian politics who had a genuine interest in academia, Smolny was initially successful. In 2021, Kudrin mobilized his connections to formalize a divorce with St. Petersburg State and create a new University of Liberal Arts and Sciences. The details of the ensuing feud are unknown, but Kudrin lost it. The Prosecutor-General of Russia declared Bard College "a threat to the fundamentals of the constitutional order and security of the Russian Federation." In 2022, Russia left the Bologna Process. A new era of military training, religious worship and freewheeling plagiarism dawned at Russian universities.

Public health and Covid-19

The three major challenges of our time – climate crisis, recurrent pandemics and militant authoritarianism – are tightly connected. One link is the emissions produced by fossil fuel. At the start of the Covid pandemic, Italian scientists noted that it was hitting mostly those areas that suffered from high industrial pollution. Atmospheric pollution weakens the immunity of the body, and CO_2 helps airborne viruses move from one individual to the next.[16] Another factor that influences transmission is the density of population: exceptions aside, the bigger the city, the worse the air.

Russia was the fourth largest emitter of CO_2 in the world, and its industrial centers were notoriously polluted. Surprisingly, Moscow did not lead the Russian charts for pollution – this honor belonged to mining cities of Siberia. However, Moscow did become the Russian center of the Covid-19 pandemic. Half of all documented cases were registered in Moscow. By the end of 2021, there were ten million confirmed cases of Covid in Russia. Excess deaths were higher than the recognized cases of Covid by a factor of three.[17] The Covid data for Russia was "absolutely unreliable," stated Alexei Kouprianov, a biologist who was promptly fired from the Higher School of Economics.[18] American political economist Anders Aslund demonstrated that Russia's response to Covid was slow: First, the Kremlin tried to hide the infection, then it delegated lockdown decisions to the regions.[19] The authorities and experts exchanged competing claims about the pandemic, but the Kremlin was always behind the curve. In April 2020, Moscow declared its first lockdown and introduced a digital pass system; the measure resulted in chaos. Angry Muscovites sabotaged actions that were introduced globally, such as the closure of restaurants and the requirement for mask-wearing. In June, the government launched a $73 billion recovery plan to counteract the pandemic's impact. All these measures imitated those that had already been introduced with some success in China and Europe, but for some reason they had hardly any effect in Russia. In 2021, the country saw its biggest annual population drop during peacetime. All that the stopmodernist state was able to do was close its borders.

In a bizarre chain of events, Russian scientists developed an effective vaccine and were the first to announce its success. Highlighting their Soviet roots, they called their product the Sputnik, named for the first satellite, launched in 1957, in a memorable victory for Soviet science. But the post-Soviet scientists failed to document their samples, and no developed country recognized Sputnik. Typically, it was a scientific achievement combined with a business failure. But the vaccine worked, the statistics were good, and people joked that getting vaccinated was the only thing one could do in Moscow free of charge. Nevertheless, there was a massive resistance to vaccination, fed by conspiracy theories and media panic. In November 2021, a poll showed that 61 percent of Russians believed that Covid-19 was a biological weapon. Targeting Western vaccines through thousands of fake social media accounts, Russian trolls spread anti-vaccination stories. Well-financed TV outlets broadcast this narrative daily for both domestic and foreign audiences. This campaign backfired: distrusting experts, millions of Russians refused to get the Sputnik. The central Moscow mall, GUM, set up a huge vaccination center among the art-deco luxury, and nurses distributed free ice cream in a bid to boost attendance. But the Sputnik was often unavailable in provincial centers. Marina Lifshits, a Russian demographer, stated in 2021: "the main element of the authorities' policy during the pandemic was a lie . . . As a result, the Russian population does not trust vaccination in principle."[20] The "chipping theory" – the idea that the vaccine included microchips that would be used for behavior control – spread on social media.[21] During the lockdowns, commoners responded to the stress and deprivation in Russian cities with sabotage and vandalism; mostly refraining from violence, they practiced its symbolic forms.[22]

Pandemic policies were difficult to impose everywhere in the world, but the high levels of popular distrust in Russia made it different from most developed countries. While medical experts emerged as public symbols of hope and solidarity elsewhere, this did not happen in Russia. When the cultural gap is unsurmountable, ordinary folk avoid complying with the rules when they can and subvert them when they can't. As with the other crises of the Anthropocene, guidance from experts on Covid was the only route to salvation. But in an unequal and anti-intellectual society, nobody – neither the commoners nor the elite – believed the experts. While the commoners saw them as a part of the elite and withdrew their trust, the actual elite of managers and officials did not count the experts as their own and did not trust them either. Distrust became a self-fulfilling prophecy: fed by bad experience, distrust led to inaction, and inaction brought sickness and death which, for the survivors, only confirmed the initial distrust.

Katechon

Invading Ukraine, the Russian rulers once again demonstrated their sheer incompetence. While their soldiers, officers and generals were dying on the random battlefields of a senseless war, the leaders rambled on about distant history, of which they were also ignorant. Their chief negotiator in the failed peace talks, the historian Vladimir Medinsky, was a proven plagiarist.[23] In the fourth month of the all-out war, Putin stated that the Russian troops were not occupying lands but "returning" them: all annexed territory had earlier belonged to Russia, and so had Ukraine.[24] But if historical primacy defined the right of capture, it was Kyiv or Stockholm that could claim Moscow, not the other way around, and Berlin could claim Kaliningrad.

Largely ignoring Putin's medieval predilections, his elite nevertheless shared his feeling of doom. The Russian world, as they knew it, was about to vanish. They had tried negotiating with their foes. They bribed and changed their governments. They learned how to conceal their failures and deny their successes. Still, their moral panic and apocalyptic despair were transparent. Putin's emotional outbursts resonated with them. "Why do we need the world if it is a world without Russia," he once said. "Death is beautiful if we die together," he said on another occasion. When Putin was young, his KGB superiors wrote in a reference that his only weakness was a "reduced sense of danger."[25] This probably helped him in his perilous career, but it also made him underestimate the risks of his all-out war. By launching the war in Ukraine and threatening a nuclear war, Putin surprised his elite like everyone else. But even before the war, many of these people had felt that their cozy world was coming to end.

Together with its ally the Russian Orthodox Church, the Kremlin revived the Soviet historiography that glorified Russian leaders who were cruel and powerful, such as Ivan the Terrible, Peter I and Stalin. Statistical analyses of Russian blogs and articles demonstrate that few names were used in proximity to Putin's more frequently than Stalin's.[26] Putin publicly mourned the USSR, but his rule was the opposite of Stalinism. Putin deindustrialized his country, was embedded in corruption and shunned internal violence. Putinism was equally distant from the Russian Empire, with its European elite, cult of honor and military victories. Explaining Putinism in terms of its Soviet heritage or as a resurgence of eternal Russia obscures the specific origins of the regime and absolves it of its crimes. Individuals and institutions, rather than a national tradition, were to blame for suppressing rallies, stealing trillions and launching the war.

The best Russian literature of the period – novels by Vladimir Sharov, Vladimir Sorokin and Dmitry Bykov – focused on the forthcoming catastrophe and the means that could (but failed to) prevent it. Combining historical details with magical fantasies, they imagined the catastrophe in cosmic or global terms, as if it were easier to imagine the end of the world than the end of Russia.[27] The mystical philosopher Alexander Dugin described Russia's mission as *katechon*, in which human effort will restrain the Antichrist and defer the End of the World.[28] An outspoken counter-modernist, Dugin joined a long intellectual tradition spanning from St. Paul to Edward Gibbon to Carl Schmitt, and taught that only an Empire could stop the End. Sanctioned in 2014, Dugin was an avid anti-Ukrainian and pro-war thinker, but his influence on Putin was unclear. He taught at Moscow State University and in military academies, but was more successful as an author. From time to time, Dugin talked about Putin critically, but Putin never mentioned Dugin in public. In August 2022, unknown assassins killed Dugin's daughter, Darya, in a Moscow car bombing; the philosopher survived.[29]

What we do know is that Dugin called for the war and Putin started it. They shared deep Soviet roots: Dugin's father was a general in military intelligence. Both were possessed by visions of the great Russian past. These historical sentiments of well-heeled Russian nationalists distinguished them from their Western colleagues: Donald Trump and even Steve Bannon, Dugin's intellectual counterpart, were rather indifferent to history. Although Putin, Dugin and their fans focused on military victories and End Times religious teachings, they were second-generation survivors of Stalinism and, more broadly, of the Soviet catastrophe. Memories of the trauma melted into its reenactment. As I demonstrated in another book, mourning is mimetic: it tends to reproduce the features of those lost and the situations connected to the loss.[30] Identification with the perpetrator is mistaken for mourning the victims. For the survivors, fear of the past turns into a compulsion to reenact the very catastrophe they have survived. The terror Putin launched in Ukraine reproduced the Great Terror of the Soviet period: recruiting soldiers among the inmates of the penal camps reproduced the practices of the Gulag, and the famine the Kremlin attempted to stage by blocking Ukrainian grain exports reenacted the Ukrainian Holodomor on a global scale. Putin launched his all-out war soon after he closed down the major institution that worked on the historical memory of Stalin's terror, Memorial International. What people fail to remember they are obliged to repeat, and what they wish to repress they keep reenacting. The unprecedented war of 2022 confirmed these old truths.

The war exposed the incompetence and anti-modern predilections of Russia's rulers better than the public sphere ever could. Cynicism instead of meritocracy, helplessness instead of dignity, and obedience instead of moral autonomy – these were the choices of those who grew up with Putin. A particularly Russian combination of abundant natural resources and a shared traumatic experience led to a sense of omnipotence: the whole world was whirling around Russia. Confronting the reality of war, that sense turned into its opposite – to impotence and the feeling of having reached a dead-end. As long as European countries kept buying Siberian fossil fuel, Putin's public lived in a utopian space. A great irony of history was that this socialist dream had been implemented by deeply conservative, far-right leaders. But it was also a bitter lesson in nemesis.

Two great songs documented two alternative views on the unfolding Russian roulette. In Robbie Williams's 'Party like a Russian' (2016), the excesses of oligarchic life were still immersed in the mysterious, seductive Russian tradition. "It takes a certain kind of man with a certain reputation / To alleviate the cash from a whole entire nation . . . I'm a modern Rasputin," sings Williams. With weird tattoos on his fists and plenty of ballerinas around, he looks content with his destiny. "Have it like an oligarch," he sings. The dancers flee and return to him in uncanny, cyclical movements. Though "there's revolution in the air," no further action follows. "It takes half the western world just to keep my ship afloat," sings the oligarch. His business secret is "seduction" – a word that Williams articulates more clearly than others – and judging by the clip, it works. In 'I Love Oil' (2013), by the Russian pop group Smash and Vengerov, a singing oligarch clumps into a glitzy bedroom carrying a barrel of oil, which he presents to his wife and kids. Then we see the wife buying a new pair of high heels: she tips open her handbag and black liquid gushes out into the hands of the shop assistant. "While there's oil in Russia, I'll be in Milan . . . I love Russia, I love oil," sings the girl. "I am this oil, I am this gas," her partner sings back. In the final scene, the former oiligarch, now a homeless beggar, pours a hatful of useless oil over his head.

Navalny

Though it had begun well before 2014, an increased suffocation of public space was the opening salvo of the war. However, the unbridled power of Putin's elite ran up against an unexpected force, which altered the clique's plans but couldn't change its taste. The name of this force was Alexei Navalny. As a lawyer, political activist, survivor of terrorism and prisoner of conscience, Navalny embodied everything that the Putin group lacked: courage, charisma and an understanding of the modern world.

In a multi-season series of online investigations viewed by millions of Russians, Navalny exposed the large-scale acts of fraud and theft committed by high-placed officials and oligarchs. He made it clear that there was more to this corruption than financial crime of absurd proportions. When a modern state turns into a cover for illegitimate wealth, it taints its citizens and infects other countries with massive distortions of justice. For politicians, the scale of state corruption makes it too big to fail; for ordinary folk, it is too large to see.

This was where Navalny's art – his visual, ironic, personalized rhetoric – came into its own. His exposés turned dozens of elected politicians and selected oligarchs into comic and hapless targets. He revealed their mansions, yachts, bodyguards and courtesans. He contrasted their senseless, tasteless luxury with their modest official salaries and the even more modest results of their executive activities. He combined screenshots of their financial statements with bird's-eye views of Palladian columns, Olympic pools and gargantuan meadows, all surrounded by huge walls and guarded by very muscular security men. For all their visual ingenuity, the key to Navalny's reports was his continuous commentary – funny, relentless and sometimes bawdy. While unveiling the palace of the then Prime Minister Dmitry Medvedev, he zoomed in on a neoclassical cottage in the middle of a lake that turned out to have been purpose-built for ducks. Rubber ducks became a symbol for Medvedev among protesting youth. In his report on a palace that allegedly belonged to Putin – and which, of course, was much bigger than Medvedev's – Navalny highlighted a gold-plated toilet brush and a ludicrous "aqua disco" with a stripper pole located in convenient proximity to the master bedroom. Though Navalny's aims were political, his means were artistic. Yes, his comments were *poshly*, a Russian word celebrated by Vladimir Nabokov that simultaneously translates as "vulgar," "posh" and "slimy." But what was truly *poshly* was Putin's neorococo palace.

Designed by an Italian architect, Lanfranco Cirillo, the building materialized the dreams of a poor Leningrad boy, whose taste had been shaped by school trips to the palaces built by the tsars and tsarinas. Working in Russia, Cirillo managed to build opulent homes for forty-three Russian billionaires from Moscow to Siberia. In March 2022, the Italian police accused him of tax evasion estimated at around 50 million euros, and confiscated valuable art and a helicopter from his villa near Brescia. In the meantime, Putin's palace was eaten by mildew; it was Cirillo's fault, but who cares? Many more millions of stolen money were wasted on its reconstruction, which remained unfinished. Corruption, like Covid, is contagious; but unlike the virus, it always defeats its own purpose.

Navalny aired his "Putin's Palace" exposé in January 2021. He had just returned to Russia from Germany, where he had received medical treatment following his poisoning in Siberia. The film was watched over 100 million times. More than 100,000 people took part in peaceful protests that stopped traffic in 110 Russian cities; three thousand of them were arrested. With the launch of the all-out war, everyone forgot about the palace, which remained home to mildew rather than, say, orphans or the wounded.

Putin always avoided mentioning the name Navalny. He referred to him instead using strange figures of speech ("the Berlin patient," "this prisoner"), as if riddled by neurotic fears or perhaps – as Moscow gossip had it – because his favorite hermit from Mount Athos had forbidden him from mentioning his enemy by name. But in the years preceding the war, politics in the capital rotated around Navalny. He put anti-corruption charges at the center of Russian politics.[31] Every scandal that implicated Moscow officials – the publication of the Panama and Pandora papers, the Marsalek Affair – was seen by the Russian public through Navalny's eyes and heard in his voice. The fact that the Kremlin had a popular and uncontrollable opponent right in the heart of Moscow only added to the suicidal despair that led the Russian rulers to war.

With his training in law and finance, his fellowship at Yale, his fluent English and hipster looks, Navalny was very much a member of the modern cosmopolitan elite. However, he spent most of his political career deconstructing this image. He talked up his "conservatism," proposed regulating the employment of marginalized migrant workers, and rallied both "nationalists" and "liberals" when marching in the streets of Moscow. Some statements he made about Crimea in 2014 were wrong and aggressive, but he later changed his views, maybe more than once.[32] He sought to permanently distance himself from the global rent-seekers, resource-traders and mega-polluters; at a time when every nation was unhappy with its elite, Russia's oily cosmopolitans appeared particularly unproductive. While oligarchs kept their families in Europe or North America, Navalny and his wife insisted on returning to Moscow. At this point, his only weapon was his own suffering body. In rejecting emigration and reinventing biopolitics, Navalny followed in the footsteps of Andrei Sakharov, the wisest of the Soviet-era dissidents, who voluntarily presented his body for humiliation and hunger. Other activists, such as Petr Pavlensky, contributed their corporeal performances – arguably, the most effective branch of modern art – to the protest culture of the 2010s. Even from his maximum-security penal colony, Navalny made the world listen to his words. Blaming Russia's "endless cycle of imperial authoritarianism," he identified "jealousy of Ukraine" as the motivating force behind Putin's war.[33]

By choosing corruption as the focus for his single-issue politics, Navalny addressed the central problem of his time while it was still invisible to others. A muckraking journalist, he was able to communicate his discoveries in the vernacular of the Russian public. Local as it was, Russian corruption defined world affairs. As an ambitious politician prepared for self-sacrifice, Navalny made it known to the world.

6

Gender and Degeneration

No single explanation for a major historical event such as a war is sufficient. Many choices, energies and gears interacted in making the war in Ukraine happen. Resource-dependency is one political-economic mechanism that certainly has explanatory power. What else other than the treasure buried in the Russian depths could have provided Putin with the funds he needed to pay his suppliers, soldiers and elite backers? There was also the bad will, lots of it: following their taste and plans, Putin, his elite and his generals consistently made pathetic – genocidal and suicidal – choices before and during the war. But in our need to understand the war, we need something more. Imagine a battle vehicle, enormous and clumsy, with a determined crew making terminal decisions. We know their names and we have already seen where the fuel came from. But there was also a *human transmission*, a chain of agency that converted the energy of the engine into the agony of the machine.

Carbon and gender

Whoever guards something, owns it. *Protego ergo obligo* was how Carl Schmitt formulated this fundamental truth of political philosophy – the extractive counterpart to Descartes' *cogito ergo sum*.[1] Just as protection from pirates was a key requirement in the tobacco and sugar trades, so the work of security personnel ranked highly in oil-dependent economies. The bottlenecks appeared not in extraction but in transportation and, especially, in securing transit routes. Oilmen rarely became heads of oil-extracting countries: their leaders were generals or intelligence agents, specialists in security.

The 1 percent of the Russian population employed in the oil and gas extraction were all men. Globally, the mining industry was second only to the military in terms of gender inequality amongst its employees.[2] In Russia, another 2 or 3 percent were employed in guarding pipelines, securing financial flows and protecting the oiligarchs' bodies and assets; they were also all men. Together, this 3–4 percent of the population accounted for half of the Russian budget. The remainder of the population – 95 percent of Russia's men and women – brought in the other half. Two classes of citizen thus emerged. The first class was the privileged all-male minority that extracted, protected and traded a valuable resource. To capture the economic, gendered and psychological character of this human type, I gave him the name *petromacho*.[3] The second class consisted of the women and men who depended on their own labor and on the redistribution of income from the oil and gas trade.

Since oil provided employment and status mostly to the men involved in extraction, transportation and security, carbon dependency was first and foremost a curse for women. Comparing the position of women in different Arab countries, Michael Ross showed that, although all these countries were Muslim, the differences among them were very significant: in some, women made up a quarter of the workforce, in others less than 5 percent. According to Ross, in countries without oil, women had more years of education and were more likely to have a job. The reason was that these countries developed other production industries – often in textiles, which generate less wealth than oil but allow for greater gender and class equality.[4] It would be interesting to apply Ross's comparative method to Russia vs. Ukraine, Azerbaijan vs. Armenia or Kazakhstan vs. Kyrgyzstan. We know that women are just as capable of working in the mining, construction and security sectors as men are. It was not nature but culture that determined gender inequalities in training and recruitment. Greed, fear and iner-tia translated petromacho's economic troubles into domestic violence, male chauvinism and homophobia.

Oppressed by the petrostate and its allies, women became heroes or symbols of resistance. In the Russian democratic movement of 2011, the Ukrainian revolution of 2014 and the Belarusian protests of 2021, many leaders were female. From Pussy Riot in Russia to Femen in Ukraine, from Yulia Tymoshenko in Kiev to Sviatlana Tsikhanouskaya in Minsk, women took symbolic leadership of protest movements. Confronting a petromacho state, rebellious manifestations of femininity became all-embracing political symbols.[5]

The nuclear family

Does modern life encourage two parents and their children to live together? Simon Kuznets, the Harvard economist of Ukrainian origin and Nobel Prize laureate, explored the evo-lution of the nuclear family on a global scale and discussed its causal connection to modernization.[6] Anatole Vishnevsky, the leading post-Soviet demographer, believed that twenty-first-century Russia had completed its transition from the premodern extended family to the modern nuclear family. This transformation involved other social institutions. Schools and nurseries helped the professional couple to care for their children. Patriarchal power turned into gender equality, with two breadwinners substituting for one another whenever needed. The elderly enjoyed their autonomy supported by savings, pensions and social services. Unfortunately, this was all too good to be true. Globally, the most common form of living in the twenty-first century is the single-person household.[7] It may eventually transpire that the idea of the nuclear family as a modern institution will be disproved as another historical myth.

Soviet industrial growth and urbanization, however, did lay a material base for the nuclear family. In its later period, the socialist state built new housing for millions of its citizens, which constituted a big improvement in comparison to factory dorms or overcrowded "communal" apartments. The new five- or nine-story blocks were built to standardized designs and contained hundreds of small apartments, though only those with a good job in a Soviet enterprise could hope to secure one. Ugly and anonymous, this housing – egalitarian, industrially produced and distributed on merit – was recognizably modern. And it was authentically Soviet: producing these ready-made blocks on assembly lines, the communists applied their thesis that all sectors of the modern economy would be better organized as industries. Mass construction made heavy use of paleomodern materials and technologies – reinforced concrete, gas welding, central heating and much else. From St. Petersburg to Vladivostok, identical projects dotted the urban landscape. In an iconic Soviet TV comedy, *The Irony of Fate* (1976), a drunken man enters an apartment in a city that, while indistinguishable from his own, is in fact hundreds of miles away – and finds happiness there.

Nobody liked these housing blocks, but they provided privacy, hygiene and a modern lifestyle to millions of people. This victory for paleomodernity was later reproduced in China, and even European communists experimented with Soviet-style mass housing. Leaving their parents, young families could live in a new and fashionable way – two parents and their children. The grandparents would remain in their village, hopefully not too far away, or in their communal apartment downtown. From the 1970s onwards, the quality of life in Soviet cities began to improve and the population grew significantly. Post-Soviet demographic tendencies were less favorable. In the same housing projects, both fertility and life expectancy decreased in the 1980s, and fell again with the collapse of the Soviet Union.

The gender gap in old age

Before the Covid-19 pandemic, Russia's spending on health care was 5.6 percent of GDP, and life expectancy was seventy-three years. Compare this to its closest Western neighbor, Finland, with 9.2 percent of GDP spent on health and an eighty-two-year life expectancy. The average age of death in Russia was one of the lowest in the world, on a level with Kirgizstan and North Korea, and much lower than in any developed country. On top of this, life expectancy in Russia also revealed gender differences that are less well known.

Russian males consistently died much younger than Russian women, and the gender mortality gap in Russia was one of the highest globally. In 2005, the average Russian woman lived for fourteen years longer than a man.[8] In a paper published a decade earlier, Harvard demographer Mark G. Field had proposed understanding this difference by analogy with war. After any war, losses within the male population are reflected as a gender gap in mortality, and Field explained Russia's demography by its defeat in the Cold War.[9] Between 2000 and 2020, Russian life expectancy at birth slowly improved, but the Covid pandemic lowered it once again. It also strengthened the gender mortality gap. According to the CIA World Factbook, life expectancy in Russia in 2021 was 65.3 for men and 77.1 years for women – a difference of almost twelve years, the highest in the world. There were eighty-six men for every 100 women in Russia in 2021 (the figures for comparison were ninety-eight in the United States and 105 in China).[10] The difference rose sharply in old age: amongst those over sixty-five, there were almost two Russian women for every man.[11] There was something specifically post-socialist in this difference. According to the World Health Organization, almost all countries with a gender mortality gap of nine years or more were post-Soviet.[12]

Although Russian men lived and worked for a shorter period than women, they earned more. In 2021, Scandinavian countries paid the most equal wages to men and women, but their neighbor Russia was ranked 81st.[13] On average, the salary of a Russian woman was 40 percent less than that of a Russian man. Women were well integrated into the labor market and held skilled jobs even more often than men, but these jobs were not better paid. It was rare for women to reach top managerial positions, and the vast majority of state officials and politicians were men. Compared even to the US, which was far from being a leader in gender equality, the difference was striking. In 2021, 10 percent of ministerial positions in Russia were held by women, compared to 46 percent in the US; 16 percent of the seats in the Russian Duma were held by women, against 27 percent of seats in the US Congress.[14] Russian women were not less educated than men – they had just as many years of schooling but this training did not translate into income or influence. By law, women retired earlier (at sixty-two, while men retired at sixty-five). Since they died later, they received a whopping twelve to fifteen more years of paid retirement than men. Many women were thus compensated for low incomes early in life with more pension payments in their senior years.

In an average Russian family, the husband would be three to five years older than his wife,[15] which meant that, after their wedding, he would have on average fifteen less years to live! Russia also topped the world for divorce rates: about 75 percent of marriages ended in divorce and the average duration of a marriage was about ten years. But even if the woman stayed married rather than divorcing, she spent a greater part of her life as a widow than as a wife. It was different in many other countries. In Italy, for example, the gender gap in longevity was 4.3 years and the average marriage was expected to last seventeen years. The average Italian woman spent more years as a wife than as a widow.

All these factors – low life expectancy, the high divorce rate, the gender gap in mortality and the gender pay gap – contributed towards the disappearance of the father. In one in three Russian families, children were raised by only one parent, usually the mother. One in three alimony payers, usually the father, refused to fulfill their obligations. In all aspects of alimony regulation Russia lagged far behind other developed countries.[16] Of all these troubling issues, the Russian government addressed only the birth rate. The Maternal Capital Program, one of Putin's personal initiatives, improved fertility by distributing direct payments to the mother for every child born. The sums were considerable, but Russia's population grew by only 1.4 percent during the whole pre-war decade. Deaths were still exceeding births, and inward migration accounted for most of the increase.[17] In the US and the UK, population growth was four times higher, even though mothers were not receiving benefits for every new birth. Addressed only to mothers, the Maternal Capital Program reinforced the asymmetry between mothers and fathers.[18] Covid-19 selectively targeted males; globally, the male death rate during the pandemic was 1.6 times that of women. Announced in September 2022, the "partial mobilization," like the earlier recruitment campaigns, targeted only men; unsurprisingly, the war in Ukraine killed many more Russian men than women. All these factors resulted in an intensification of the gender mortality gap.

Before and during the war, fertility in Russia was in free fall: fewer children per day were born in Russia during the first six months of the war than during the two years of Covid. By September 2022, the birth rate in the country was at an historical low. Apparently, many who might have been thinking about conceiving the previous January knew the future better than the experts.

Fatherlessness

Unfortunately, the issue of fatherlessness – or of the matrifocal family, as anthropologists call it – has been largely neglected by social science. The Frankfurt School theorists mentioned the absence of the father as a possible precondition for the emergence of an authoritarian personality. After World War II, the German psychoanalyst Alexander Mitscherlich wrote that, with the number of fathers dead, drunk or overworked, the postwar generation was "nobody's children." While the father shaped the child's conscience or "critical instinct," fatherlessness led to narcissism and aggression. The result was a mass society, which Mitscherlich imagined as a crowd of siblings deprived of their fathers.[19] Anthropologists believed that matrifocal family was characteristic of the Afro-Caribbean peoples; its connection to the post-socialist condition had not been acknowledged.[20]

The fatherless family structure has, however, been extensively studied in psychological literature. Dozens of works show that a fatherless childhood lowers test scores, school grades, educational aspirations and years of schooling. Children who grow up without a father are more likely to have emotional issues as students, to suffer from low self-esteem and to have issues with their peers. A comparative study of students in thirty-three developed countries demonstrated that fatherless students more often blame others for their failures. Another stream of research looked at multigenerational households. The children of these households, which are mostly poor, tended to be cognitively and emotionally disadvantaged. Students who lived with at least one grandparent scored lower in numeracy and tended to blame others for their failures (what psychologists call "external locus of control"). In almost every developed country, research showed that growing up in a full nuclear family was optimal for children.[21] In highlighting the importance of the father, these results reflected the intrinsic connection between the nuclear family and capitalism at its "developed" stage.

In Russia, families were rarely full and rarely nuclear. Jennifer Utrata, an anthropologist from Berkeley, interviewed single mothers in central Russia. "Normalized gender crisis is simply the way things are there," she wrote in 2015.[22] One explanation for the relatively short lives of Russian men was their tendency towards binge drinking, heavy smoking, high-fat diets and lack of exercise.[23] But unhealthy lifestyles were also the norm for many Russian women. But even if unemployed or impoverished, women still have their children and grandchildren to take care of.[24] For them, childcare was both a burden and a refuge. Men avoided their families and children far more often than women, and this crucial difference was connected to men's shorter lives.

Factors of degeneration

For decades, scholars knew about Russia's demographic catastrophe and were puzzled by it. Since the depopulation uniquely occurred in peacetime, Western scholars attributed it to the collapse of the Soviet welfare system. But the causality went in the opposite direction. It was not that the end of the Cold War led to Russia's depopulation. Rather, it was Russia's degeneration that led to the new war.

Degeneration is a strong word; widespread in the early twentieth century, it is making a comeback a hundred years later.

I use it along with the weaker term "depopulation," but degeneration foregrounds a change in quality as well as in quantity. The leading Russian demographer Anatoly Vishnevsky wrote in 2003: "A very real mortal challenge has been sent to Russia, but nobody so far has dared take it up."[25] The leading American demographer Murray Feshbach wrote in 2008: "The [Russian] nation is not just sick but dying."[26] His colleague, Nicholas Eberstadt, called Russia's depopulation a "terrible mystery." In his view, "the health disaster underway in Russia is not only outside Western experience; in important ways, it may still be beyond Western understanding."[27] The causes were deeper than social diseases such as tuberculosis, alcoholism, AIDS and, more recently, Covid. Historical traumas, a general lack of trust and the debilitating experience of many Russians in prisons and military barracks also played a role.

One factor of degeneration was the rotting of the political economy. Russia's decline continued the Soviet past. Like the enclosures during the Industrial Revolution in England, the Soviet collectivization deprived peasants of land while industrialization drove them into the cities. Beautifully described by the Russian economist Alexander Chayanov, pre-revolutionary Russian peasants were stuck in non-profit, equilibrium-oriented "moral economies." By force, the Bolsheviks transformed peasant communities into industrial collectives that preached enthusiasm and practiced obedience. Trained and employed in these collectives, settlers and their children lost their farming culture, folklore and identities. Instead, they acquired disciplinary and technological skills: they became a proletariat. The peasants resisted fiercely, at first by force of arms during the Civil War, then through sabotage, and finally with the despair and apathy that were typical of the Russian village. Millions perished, but millions more became obedient workers in Soviet factories or neat clerks in Soviet offices. But the concomitant loss of agricultural productivity was devastating. Despite having some of the best agricultural land on earth, the

USSR could not feed itself. The Food Program adopted at the 1982 Communist Party Congress relied on massive purchases of grain from North America in exchange for oil from Western Siberia, with German mediation in the triangular trade. From the Western perspective, this was the first "oil-for-food program" to provide life support to a belligerent petrostate. The Atlantic West later adopted similar programs in restructuring trade with Iraq, Iran and Venezuela.

Converted into rubles and injected into the domestic economy, petrodollars had to return to the treasury. For the government, encouraging alcohol consumption was an easy way to boost its ruble revenue. In the late Soviet period, both the people and the state became drug addicts. The people got addicted because alcohol, even though heavily taxed, remained the cheapest source of pleasure. The state got addicted because it relied on alcohol taxation to return the money it had invested in welfare. In Russia, alcohol was counter-modern, as the drunken soldiers who took part in the Bucha massacre of 2022 fully demonstrated.

In 2003, Putin unveiled an ambitious plan for expanding the national economy: the goal was 7 percent growth a year for the decades ahead. Budgeted by Putin's economic advisor, Andrei Illarionov, the plan foresaw a doubling in the size of the economy by 2013 and a quadrupling after that. As a result, Russia would emerge as the world's fifth largest economy by 2020. In fact, that year the Russian economy was ranked eleventh. Mismanagement, corruption, wars and sanctions had all taken their toll. Nobody in the Kremlin, and very few Western experts, planned for or predicted these losses. But the Russian population felt them in advance, and responded preemptively. Comparing the year on year changes in the Russian economy with the changes in population, one sees that, although the curves were similar, demographic decline usually preceded economic decline. Taken together, the figures suggest that people were refusing to reproduce because they distrusted the promises of their leaders or were protesting against their decisions. The birth rate was the ultimate manifestation of public opinion. There was no trust, no security, no future – and therefore, no kids.

Albert O. Hirschman, a pioneer of developmental economics, argued that when people are unhappy and disloyal to their leaders, they have two options, voice or exit.[28] In the 1990s, the Russian people had a voice – an opportunity to express their discontent in the public sphere and sometimes in democratic elections. That voice was silenced when Putin came to power in 2000. Building his institutions of power, the new president launched his first battles against modernity. In response, many Russians and non-Russians left the country. Others were sapped of their desire to bring children into the world. Russia's depopulation was an exercise of the people's right to exit. Insecure, unhealthy people died young; unhappy, hopeless people refused to reproduce. Demographic processes proactively responded to political events.

In 2022, Russia came 75th in the world ranking of self-reported happiness, on par with Tajikistan. The list was topped by Finland, and all European countries were ranked as happier than Russia.[29] Critical demographers spoke then of "deaths of despair," observed particularly in former mining regions and rust belts around the world, from Eastern Europe to North America.[30] In Russia, there were also millions of abortions of despair.

From the late Soviet period onwards, Russia was a world leader in abortions. Seemingly concerned, the state attempted to discourage them by various means, from a ban in the last years of Stalinism to the "Maternal Capital" payments of Putin's era. In 1991, the average Russian woman had 3.4 abortions in her lifetime; by 2014, this number had decreased by a factor of four. However, no burst of fertility was achieved. The number of births per year slowly approached the number of terminations but exceeded it only in 2007. Russia was starting and ending its wars, but Russians were still removing their embryos at the same rate at which they were dying of natural causes. In 2022, the number of terminations per woman in Russia – a country in which abortion was almost never talked about – was four times higher than in the US, where it was a central political issue.

Domestic violence was another indicator of dysfunctional family life. In 1999, the *American Psychologist* journal reported that the frequency of domestic violence in Russia exceeded Western figures by a factor of four. Every year, about 15,000 women were murdered by their male partners, and Russia's per capita rate of feminicide surpassed that of all other countries.[31] Moreover, in 2017, Russia decriminalized domestic battery. A man who beat his wife or children could now only be punished with a fine.[32] When the rate of physical assaults, stalking and other forms of domestic violence rose sharply during the Covid lockdowns, there was no legislation to deal with them.[33]

During the Fat Years, Russia attracted about ten million migrants, most of them young males from Central Asia and China. Coming to Moscow and Southern Siberia, they were lured by the relatively high wages for non-qualified laborers. The authorities encouraged this immigration as long as it boosted their revenue. Without inward migration, the depopulation crisis would have been much worse. On the other hand, migrants competed with unqualified locals, increasing unemployment and discontent. After the occupation of Crimea in 2014 and the devaluation of the ruble in 2016, millions of migrant workers left Russia, most of them broke.

Five million people left the country during the first twenty years of Putin's rule; 300,000 left after the war resumed in February 2022, and about 200,000 left in response to the "partial mobilization" in September that year. Many of these emigrants were skilled professionals – IT experts, journalists, engineers, etc. Putin's administration did not mind losing its young and educated subjects because it saw them as a source of social protest, and also thought they were not needed anyway. This brain drain only added to the Russian depopulation problem, in terms of both quantity and quality.

Babushkas

In the early twenty-first century, the lack of affordable housing for young couples was a global issue, but Russia's demographic was again unique. Unable to buy or rent a place of their own, Russian women and men cohabited with the older generation, which usually meant a widowed mother. One poll found that 27 percent of young Russians lived with their parents, which roughly corresponded to the European average; but other estimates went as high as 80 percent.[34] In addition, many families received regular help from granny, even if they didn't live with her. Together, these phenomena led to the grandmother-dominated family. A typical such family consisted of the *babushka* (granny) taking care of one child, with a largely absent father and an overburdened, full-time working mother. This was a *post-socialist family*, neither nuclear nor extended. It fit within a small, Soviet-style apartment and matched the overdisciplined Soviet-style schools. To an anthropologist, Russian families resembled South African families in that the mothers often became responsible for breadwinning while the grandmothers took over childcare and housework.[35] In both countries, extreme forms of inequality such as serfdom and apartheid had shaped the life of later generations. Poverty and exploitation forced many households to retain, or restore, the extended multigenerational family. The folkish Russia of Alexander Chayanov survived and reconstituted itself due to this mechanism.

Exercising matriarchal power while also transmitting the patriarchal values of the larger society, the *babushka* cultivated the traditional norms of discipline and obedience. In the poorest households, the granny could be also important because of her pension, and her role in private gardening and informal trade. As real estate prices skyrocketed, mortgages with 10–18 percent interest rates did not help. Pensions remained very low. From kindergartens to hospices, social services remained unavailable. The lack of mass housing forced the generations into an informal contract: the young couple lived in the inherited household and enjoyed free childcare provided by the granny; in exchange, the couple took care of the granny's financial and healthcare needs. As a result, the post-socialist, three-generational family saved the Russian state from having to spend billions on kindergartens and retirement homes, which would have had to be subsidized by the taxpayer. Saving on social services and passionate about conservative values, Putin's gerontocracy was a perfect counterpart to the *babushka*-dominated family.

Unlike the father, however, the grandmother could not provide a role model for the children. Imitating or contesting her were not attractive options that moved them forward. In a patriarchal and aging society, the grandmother was excluded from active life. Mediated through her, routine novelties such as contraceptives, healthy diets, internet skills or recycling habits arrived slowly. Coming from school and peers rather than from family, these innovations were perceived with suspicion as foreign or temporary. Depending on the extent of her charm and power, the granny imposed her premodern ideas and patterns of behavior – communitarian tradition, risk-aversion, external locus of control – over the heads of the parents and straight onto the grandchildren. Skipping a whole generation of absent fathers and overburdened mothers, granny-led families slowed cultural development. A cultural shift that would have taken thirty years had it passed from parents to children took sixty years when passed from granny to grandchildren. Substituting for the disappeared fathers, granny power thus proved to be an effective and durable weapon against modernity.

The grandfather rule

Bullying in Russian schools and the hazing of young recruits in the army added to the misery of Russia's fatherless males. In 2019, Ramil Shamsutdinov, a twenty-year-old soldier in Siberia, gunned down eight fellow soldiers. During his induction into the service he was tortured by other soldiers and officers, and threatened with rape. "The officers promised to turn me out. They warned me that, like, they'll rape me. I know they'd turned all the other young ones out [who had been raped] before me. If that evening was my turn, I had nowhere to go, what should I have done?" Shamsutdinov reportedly said.[36] Both sides, the rapists and the raped, understood these acts not as sexual but as pedagogical: the rapists did not acknowledge their pleasure but talked of instilling obedience and discipline among the raped. Soldiers who had been raped on their first year of service would go on to do the same to the new recruits a year later. This barbaric initiation was called *dedovschina*, the grandfather rule: young soldiers identified with the grandfathers they probably had never known and probably would never be. The idea that grandfathers rape their grandsons is of course monstrous. But it did motivate this ritual, one of the most unusual games of power in the modern world.

In premodern society, initiation rituals embodied underlying values and passed them from generation to generation; by remaining in obscurity, these rituals resisted the advance of modernity that would destroy them. The few scholars who studied hazing in the Russian army and prisons revealed that this particular ritual originated in Soviet institutions but intensified following their reform.[37] Mixing up hugely different feelings and actions in a traumatic experience, the "grandfather soldiers" created an emotional chaos of *dedovschina* that foreshadowed the political chaos of Putinism. The ubiquity of rape in the military was perversely connected to the homophobia typical of the grandfathers who held power in Russia. While projecting homosexuality onto an imagined West, the elders in power condoned the sexual violence against the young recruits. In their youth, some of these militant homophobes had experienced rape in one role or another, or both.

Ulrich Beck wrote that industrial modernity produced "a half-modern, half-feudal society," with public institutions and industries that were mostly modern and a family life that was anti-modern.[38] This two-tier or even bicameral modernity offers a helpful image, but in the Russian case the relations between the two parts need more attention. A stereotypical father comes home and talks about his work over dinner: this is the children's window onto the big world, their most important connection to modernity. A stereotypical grandmother shares her memories of the distant past with her grandchildren and tells them archaic folkish fairytales. Many grandmothers no doubt gave genuine love and care to their grandchildren, but they could not substitute for the fathers in stimulating competition, conscience and moral autonomy. The flight of men from the family created an inter-generational loop that helped women to survive together, pushed the remaining fathers to the margins of social life, and increased the gender difference in longevity.

The symmetry between the pseudo-nuclear Russian family and the pseudo-democratic Russian politics was striking. Both were monological and monopolistic, gerontocratic and backward-looking, rent-seeking and violent. The impoverished grandmothers of the Russian suburbs were natural allies of the super-wealthy grandfathers in the Kremlin, who shared the inherent conservatism of the three-generation family. Dominated by the widowed grandmother, the family was matriarchal. Dominated by the lonely Kremlin elder, the state was patriarchal. As if connected in a sexless but polygamous marriage, these institutions complemented and supported each other through a variety of economic and cultural strings.

7

Putin's War

There were many reasons for Russia's self-destruction, and each of them warrants scrutiny. Theology teaches that vices cannot be deduced from one another: greed is separate from wrath and both differ from gluttony. Tyranny is also deadly and irreducible to other kinds of evil. Putinism was a complex evil and no single explanation for it is sufficient. Corrupted and corrupting, aggressive and elusive, it turned foes into friends – and friends into foes – with an ease that made modernity more liquid than ever. In Ukraine, it met its retribution. A wiser tyrant would have deferred his inevitable end for another few years, even a decade. Impatient and bored, Putin was the unexpected nemesis of Putinism.

A war between generations

Every war reverses the natural order of things: sons die and fathers mourn, not the other way around. Every war brings the problem of generations to the fore. Ivan Turgenev wrote his *Fathers and Sons*, the paradigmatic literary analysis of the problem, in the aftermath of the Crimean War; Karl Mannheim wrote his "The Problem of Generations," the paradigmatic scholarly analysis, in the aftermath of World War I.

The political regime that launched the war in Ukraine was as gerontocratic as in the last years of the Soviet Union. By 2022, Putin had spent longer in power than Brezhnev (twenty-two years vs. sixteen), ceding the record for Kremlin longevity only to Stalin (twenty-nine years). Comparing the Russian and the Ukrainian leaderships at the outset of the war, the enormous difference in age is striking. Putin, aged seventy, could easily be the forty-four-year-old Zelensky's father, and the same was true of almost every Russian member of cabinet in comparison to their Ukrainian counterparts.

The conditions for the war grew out of the conflicts, in Russia and Ukraine, between the septuagenarian boomers and later generations. A major divide in any country, generations are shaped by their historical experiences more than by their dates of birth, and the rupture of 1991 established a huge difference between generations. In both Ukraine and Russia, the cohort difference between the generations was larger than the ethnic difference between peers of the same generation. The distribution of power in terms of age makes this very clear. Born in the wake of World War II, Russia's rulers were deeply rooted in the Soviet period. These boomers went to Soviet schools and started their careers in Soviet collectives. Of the eighty-two Russian billionaires listed by Forbes in 2022, almost all of them belonged to that generation of Soviet boomers.[1] Peers of Putin and his regime, this tiny elite of oligarchs and officials amassed enormous wealth during the Fat Years, a decade that started after 2000. The Ukrainian leaders, on the other hand, knew about the Soviet era only from history books. Among the twenty-three members of the Ukrainian Cabinet in 2022, only four were older than fifty. Among the thirty-one members of the Russian Cabinet, only six were younger than fifty. In 1991, the future Russian minister of foreign affairs, Sergey Lavrov, was forty-one – exactly the same age his Ukrainian counterpart Dmitro Kuleba was in 2022. The Russo-Ukrainian War – a war between two neighboring peoples of similar languages and diverging cultures – was a *war between generations: an Oedipus conflict of enormous scale.*

In Russia, Zelensky's peers were a lost generation. Educated during the decade of decline in the 1990s, they felt resentment towards their more successful predecessors among the boomers. Mikhail Anipkin, a Russian-British sociologist, compared the Russian political life of the pre-war period to a theater: Born in the 1950s, the boomers occupied the stage and performed their endless play. In the wings were the millennials born in the 1980s, helplessly waiting for their turn on stage. Uninterested, generation X – the lost people born in the 1970s – drank at the bar. The youngsters from the most recent generation whistled in protest, but the *babushka* ushers kicked them out.[2]

The unbearable lightness of Western pundits

Putin's invasion of Ukraine shocked and confused the world. Even naming the event posed a problem. Declaring his war on Ukraine on the night of February 24, 2022, Putin did not once use the word "war" and barely mentioned Ukraine. Instead, he informed the world that he begun "a special military operation." Wars have their laws and customs – Putin's operation had none. The collective voice of the West chose to call it "the Russian invasion of Ukraine." But the Ukrainians fought a very real war, and Ukraine had as much agency as Russia. This equality should be reflected in the concept. My choice of denomination is the Russo-Ukrainian War (2014–?), which evokes the Russo-Japanese (1904–5) and Russo-Polish (1919–21) wars – both lost by Russia.

Putin knew perfectly well that he was starting a war, but he hoped his "special operation" label would function as a stealthy conceptual weapon, passing undetected on public radars. Clearly, he was mistaken. Russia's barbaric war brought global condemnation and Ukraine got the help it needed. At first, however, some leading voices described Ukraine as a failed state and a sort of strategic nuisance, one that had been meddling in the affairs of the real players. Prejudice, ignorance and material interests were all in evidence at this point.

On the day of invasion, Christian Lindner, the powerful German minister of finance, told the Ukrainian ambassador to his country that Kyiv would fall the next day; the ambassador, Andrij Melnyk, tried to argue, then wept. A few weeks later, Lindner was swearing that Germany would never stop supporting Ukraine.[3] Adam Tooze, an economic historian at Columbia University, wrote in January 2022: "What makes Ukraine into the object of Russian power is not just its geography, but the division of its politics, the factional quality of its elite and its economic failure."[4] In other countries, competition within the elite is called democracy – why did the Ukrainian elite have to be monolithic? Ukraine's economic growth during the post-Soviet decades was three times lower than Russia's, Tooze stated. He failed to mention that Russia's growth was secured by fossil fuels that polluted the world and Ukraine's by the labor of its farmers and IT workers. In the era of the Anthropocene, applauding the superiority of oil and gas revenues was a little shortsighted. If Russia showed strong economic growth and Ukraine did not, did that confirm the superiority of Russia or discredit the indicators of growth?

A week before the invasion, Katrina vanden Huevel, the influential publisher of *The Nation* magazine, suggested that "Ukraine is the closest thing Europe has to a failed state." She claimed (wrongly) that three American presidents had refused to provide military support to Ukraine because it "was not worth defending." Finally, she proposed "a deal that guarantees Ukraine's sovereignty and independence in exchange for guaranteeing its neutrality,"[5] forgetting that Ukraine had already given up its nuclear weapons and acquired sovereignty and independence thirty years earlier – all guaranteed by the United States, Russia and other countries.

In his well-informed book on the subject, Thane Gustafson, professor at Georgetown University, analyzed the likely impact of the energy transition on Russia's economy. In the early 2030s, Russia's exports of oil, gas and coal would decline sharply, and by 2050 its total exports would be reduced by half.[6] This is a bleak picture, wrote Gustafson, "a major turning point for Russia." Gustafson published his book just a year before the war. What he predicted for 2050 occurred in 2022, and the causality was different: it was not climate action that caused the fall in Russian exports, but Russian aggression that accelerated the global transition.

Predictions differ from explanations, and prophets from scholars. In times of war, predictions materialize quickly enough for people to remember them and judge their authors. In January 2022, Niall Ferguson, a popular historian, compared Putin to Peter I, the founder of the Russian Empire. Like Peter, Putin would win his own battle of Poltava, Ferguson wrote. Russia's imperial history, he speculated, "inspires today's Tsar Vladimir . . . much more than the dark chapters of Stalin's reign of terror." Indeed, a couple of months later, Putin publicly compared himself to Peter I. Ferguson understood Putin but failed to understand his war. Ignoring Russia's economic and demographic problems and believing in its easy victory, Ferguson stated that Ukraine would "receive no significant military support from the West." Putin would win his war, and Ferguson his punchline: "Do not be surprised if [Putin's] victory parade takes place in Poltava," he wrote just before the invasion.[7] As the war turned into a major disappointment for Putin's admirers, Ferguson was less bullish: "What makes history so hard to predict . . . is that most disasters come out of left field," he wrote in early March. Whether left field or right, the historian reaffirmed his license: "The language people speak in the corridors of power . . . is not economics or politics. It is history." Thus, Ferguson predicted that Mariupol would fall in a few days, Biden's administration would not support Ukraine, and since most Russian leaders died of natural causes, so would Putin.[8] We know that at least some of his predictions did not come true. There was definitely no parade in Poltava.

In June 2022, John Mearsheimer, professor at the University of Chicago, stated that the reason for Putin's war was the threat posed by NATO: if Ukraine joined, Russia would suffer "existentially," and this justified Russia's actions.[9] A month or two passed, and this "political realism" was refuted by real politics. Finland and Sweden joined NATO because of Putin's war. With their accession, NATO was much closer to Russia's vital centers than it would have been had Ukraine ever succeeded with its application to join the alliance. Any "realist" could have seen this was about to happen, but not Mearsheimer.

This chain of events is a great example of political nemesis. Putin was so afraid of NATO that he ending up bringing it to the gates of his hometown of St. Petersburg. The same tale of nemesis unfolded with the gas pipelines. Putin wanted his gas to bypass Ukraine so much that he built two hugely expensive pipelines under the Baltic Sea. One was completed but did not become operational because of the war, while the other was barely functioning. In September 2022, somebody – maybe the Russians, maybe their enemies – blew up both pipelines. In the meantime, Russian gas kept flowing through Ukraine.

Whatever the false predictions, the Ukrainians were valiant on the battlefield and artful in diplomacy. Blending his political and theatrical skills, President Zelensky produced a daily show in his capital, bestowing popularity on some Western leaders and refusing hospitality to others. From a nonplace that once required the article "the" as if it had no proper name, Ukraine had turned into the political center of the world.

The future is like a Rorschach inkblot: people respond to uncertainty by projecting their desires onto it. Neither pundits nor prophets know the future, but those who predict it reveal themselves. There is no worse mistake for pundits than to make the wrong predictions during a war. We learn of their desires, and they are laughable.

Germany's Finlandization

Curiously, the "realists" launched a project of Finlandizing Ukraine at the very moment Finland abandoned its special relations with Russia. First put forward in 1961 by the German historian Richard Löwenthal, the concept of Finlandization was the logical conclusion of Cold War *realpolitik*. After the Winter War with the Soviet Union (1939–40) and World War II, Finland lost one fifth of its industry and more than a tenth of its population. Having accepted a partial demilitarization, Finland became the Soviet Union's largest trade partner. Astonishingly, it also accepted various forms of Soviet control that even included the censorship of books in Finnish public libraries. Later, the Soviet Union added carrots to sticks, offering guaranteed prices for Russian oil and buying Finnish products in a process that resembled barter.[10] In the 1960s, these exchanges developed into a jointly administered "ruble clearing account": transactions could be made as long as total trade balanced in each five-year period. In the 1980s, falling oil prices weakened this barter system and caused an economic crisis in Finland. The country found that its technologies were obsolete and its banks non-competitive, and that even its farms were failing in the European market.

Something similar happened in Germany with the start of the Russo-Ukrainian War. The country had been developing its imports and exports in line with the *Wandel durch Handel* ("change through trade") principle. Some Germans called this idea Kantian, but it was mercantilist; more importantly, it never worked. When the British Empire sold opium to China, or the

US sold grain to the Soviet Union, they made lots of money but saw little progress in their partners. Clearly, the energy trade with Russia was profitable for Germany, but why did they see cancelling it as a full-scale catastrophe? It was only trade, after all; if it relied on competitive prices, then one trading partner could be replaced by another. But the prices Russia set for Germany were not competitive. Insulated from the global market by fixed pipelines and long-term contracts, German corporations received big discounts, which grew even bigger every time prices went up. These accumulated discounts were so significant that in April 2022 German businesses warned that the termination of Russian trade would lead to inflation, recession and a trade deficit. Deutsche Bank estimated that the losses would amount to $220 billion, a sum larger than the much-discussed German trade surplus in 2021.[11] Like Finland in the 1970s and Ukraine in the 2000s, Germany in the 2010s was *resource-dependent by proxy.*

Neither German industry nor the global public recognized that the reason for the country's surplus had been cheap Russian gas; everyone preferred to talk about the efficiency of its banks and the productivity of its workers. In fact, these workers were underpaid and the infrastructure decaying, but German industrialists continued to channel their surpluses elsewhere.[12] In a resource-bound country, as we have seen, financial results do not depend on the population or infrastructure, and the money does not return to the people or the land.

The Russian pipelines insulated German businesses from the outside world, with its gaiamodern challenges of decarbonization and authoritarianism. Enjoying access to the pipelines, the German flagships of technical progress were making guaranteed profits based on low energy costs, stability of supplies and long-term planning. This was particularly significant when global markets were in turmoil, as they often had been over the previous two decades. The historical experience of Finland helps us to understand these new facts of European life. Extending the Soviet practice of Finlandizing its neighbors, the Russo-German energy trade was closer to a barter clearing system than to a free market. Russia's dominance in this trade was overwhelming. It owned not only the Siberian gas, but also the pipelines on land and under the sea, and even the gas reservoirs on German territory. Despite Germany's success in developing renewable energy sources, these paleomodern structures blocked its adjustment to the new modernity of the Anthropocene.

Genocide and fetishism

What's worse, malice or mismanagement? The correct answer is, a mismanaged malice. Though the military aspects of the war were badly mismanaged by the Russian authorities, its genocidal aspects were preplanned and intentional. Russian actions in Ukrainian cities and villages included mass murders and deportations combined with the intentional destruction of cultural objects and institutions (monuments, museums, theaters, etc.), educational facilities and history textbooks. This is what Raphael Lemkin, who studied in Lviv and watched how the Soviets engineered famine in fertile Ukraine, called barbarity and vandalism; in 1944, he named this combination "genocide."[13] As he wrote, "genocide has two phases: one, destruction of the national pattern of the oppressed group; the other, the imposition of the national pattern of the oppressor."[14] He continued by saying that the oppressed group could be either exterminated or allowed to remain on the land. The latter we would call "colonization." In both its variations, external and internal, colonization often led to mass murder.[15]

But there is a catch. In most cases of colonization, the oppressor and the oppressed were separated by various distances and differences – geographical, racial, economic, cultural, religious, linguistic, etc. These differences shaped the patterns of imperial governance. Perceived differences in the color of skin provided grounds for racism. Differences in economic and technological development made the empire militarily superior and capable of exploiting the colonies. Many of these differences were constructed by the colonizers in their interest, while others were real and accessible to independent observation. Historians found such situations in the genocidal actions committed against the natives of America or Siberia, or in the imperial wars in Africa and Asia. In the long and tortured history of Russo-Ukrainian relations, perceived differences were in short supply. Even the aggressor had a hard time putting his finger on them.[16]

Where two "national patterns" are not that dissimilar, markers of difference between them can be artificially constructed: if not languages, then dialects and accents; if not different religions, then different costumes or fashions; if not skin color, then different ways of cutting hair or shaving beards. These minor differences then grow into fetishes: they become more important than the bigger and more profound similarities, and come to define life or death. There is no genocide without distinct "national patterns," but the fetishized differences between those patterns would be negligible for any other purpose than genocide. *There is a fetish beneath any genocide.*

In the Bible there is a story about how the Gileadites fought against a neighboring people, the Ephraimites. Those Ephraimites who fled and were captured had to pass a phonetic test – pronouncing the Hebrew word "Shibboleth." For saying "Sibboleth" instead, forty-two thousand Ephraimites were killed (Judges 12:5–6). Citing this story, Victor Shklovsky, the Russian-Jewish scholar who took part in World War I and saw its aftermath in Ukraine, commented: "The Bible repeats itself in a curious way . . . In the Ukraine [*sic*!] I saw a Jewish boy. He could not look at the corn without trembling. He told me: When they were killing us in the Ukraine they needed to check whether the person they were about to kill was Jewish. They asked him: 'Say *kukuruza* (corn).' Sometimes, he said: *Kukuruzha*. They killed him."[17]

There is not much difference between this use of phonetics and the Nazi method of identifying Jews by circumcision: obviously neither of these markers warrant murder. Other genocides followed the same logic of identifying minor differences. Historians know that the Armenian genocide of 1915–17 and the Bosnian genocide of 1995 cannot be explained by religious hostilities between Muslims and Christians. The Young Turks – mostly intellectuals and military officers – who came to power in the Ottoman Empire in 1908 aimed to secularize their country. At the outset of their campaign, the Armenian radicals – also secular intellectuals and military officers – supported the Young Turks and took part in their movement. There had been no genocide throughout the long centuries during which Turks and Armenians lived side by side in separate religious communities; the genocide only occurred after their religious differences had been mostly eliminated.

The internal terror in the Soviet Union, which spanned three decades and only ended with Stalin's death in 1953, was equivalent to genocide even though the perpetrators and the victims often belonged to the same ethnicity and class and shared the same ideology. It even happened that an interrogator would be arrested and then meet one of his former victims in the same camp. For Bosnians and Serbs in the late twentieth century, their religious and cultural differences did not play the role they played in the past.[18] The same could safely be said about the Russians and Ukrainians when they lived side by side – in both Russia and Ukraine – before the disastrous war of 2022.

The absence of meaningful differences does not decrease the scale or the cruelty of the mass murder. On the contrary, the lesser the differences the greater the genocide. The smaller the chosen differences are, the more the genocide approaches a collective suicide. Indeed, this analogy with suicide has been noted in many historiographies of genocide, from Somalia and Cambodia to the Soviet Union and the Russian invasion of Ukraine.

In *Civilization and its Discontents* Sigmund Freud wrote: "it is precisely communities with adjoining territories, and related to each other as well, who are engaged in constant feuds and in ridiculing each other ... I gave this phenomenon the name of the 'narcissism of minor differences,' a name that does not do much to explain it."[19] The latter is probably true, but I see something valuable in Freud's idea. If people are perceived as different, they can be used and abused, and the abuse would be seen in terms of economics rather than politics. If you treat another person (or animal) as a means, then they will usually be a creature very different from you, and it is this difference that allows you to maintain this instrumental relation; but if you see another person as an end, then this person will probably be similar to you, and evoke either love or hatred. Political relations emerge among those who are similar.

Attempting to make sense of the Balkan genocides, Canadian historian Michael Ignatieff invoked this old Freudian concept of minor differences.[20] Narcissism turned small differences into grand narratives, which then led to mass murder. This does not, however, explain why and how two neighboring and similar peoples become a genocidal couple. Many human groups are similar, but this does not lead them to kill one another. Genocide does not function as a causal chain of events that starts with a small difference and ends with a mass grave. The opposite is true. Mass murders happen for reasons that have nothing to do with ethnic differences, big or small. But after they have taken place, the survivors on both sides explain the slaughter by converting their small, negligible differences into grand, overwhelming narratives.

There are multiple differences between human groups, and the number of small differences is infinite. Looking at racial differences, Critical Race Theory deconstructs them by arguing that they have no objective referents – they are all created by cultural perceptions. One could say that Critical Race Theory works as an exact antidote to the "narcissism of small differences": the former turns big differences, as they are perceived in racist society, into minor collaterals of cultural interactions; the latter turns small differences into decisive factors that, for a murderous group, determine the difference between life and death. There is no "objective" metric that could define which differences are small (e.g. accents) and which differences are big (races or generations). They are all constructed, contingent and fluid. In the way of structuration, political agency can turn any set of human differences into a genocidal matter.

According to Lemkin, the reason for genocide is the oppressors' striving to establish their own order in the occupied lands. The murderers want to get power, property and recognition from their own kind and from neighboring peoples. Differences are in the eyes of the beholder, but if one person has power he can impose his perception on others. Putin, his state and his army were determined to destroy the "national pattern" of the Ukrainians and replace it with the "national pattern" of the Russians. The perceived differences were small, but the political results were enormous. In some ways the Russians and the Ukrainians were so similar that no Shibboleth test would have differentiated them. But in other ways they were vastly different. The striking difference between the generations in power was, from Putin's perspective, impossible to acknowledge. The Russians and Ukrainians are the same people, Putin said on the eve of his assault in 2022. To identify the enemy amongst a people who looked and sounded like themselves, the Russian soldiers couldn't rely even on accents – many of them had similar ways of pronouncing Russian words. Having no other clue, the Russian soldiers on the checkpoints searched people for "Nazi tattoos" – anyone who had anything interpretable as such on their skin was beaten or killed. And those who sent these soldiers to Ukraine developed their own marks of difference.

The story of Z

The war against Ukraine was as senseless as any other genocide: it could not bring Russia any political or economic gain,
and it did not. It was only comprehensible within a frame-
work combining classic Russian imperialism with a specifically
post-Soviet revanchism. But there was also a third element to
the mix: fetishism. The Russian losses were huge and predict-
able, but they did not matter. What mattered was the fetish:
a Ukrainian territory whose only value came from the idea
that it used to be "ours" and should be regained. Supposedly,
this would have brought glory, ecstasy or some other form of
satisfaction to the Russian president, his elite and their people.

Nobody understands a fetishistic desire but the fetishist.
Moreover, different fetishists don't understand each other:
one worships a heel and another an elbow. However, fetishism is a venerable concept; both Marx and Freud loved it.
Why does anyone take pleasure from the proverbial heel?
It's incomprehensible, and the victim, the owner of the heel,
is as dumbfounded as anyone else. None of this matters to
the fetishist; he seeks pleasure above all else. It is exactly this
disproportion between a part and a whole that constitutes
fetishism. Crimea was such a heel and so was the Donbas.
In national catastrophes of this scale, there is always this
irrational, incomprehensible core. German historians of the
Holocaust call it a "civilizational rupture." It is important to
analyze imperialism and revanchism, two comprehensible
sources of both catastrophes, but it would be wrong to see in
them the whole picture. Your foe, the fetishist, would be happy
to deceive you in this way.

Militant and potentially genocidal, fetishist culture is full of
contradictions. When the emperor is a fetishist his poets write
odes and his sculptors erect monuments to the fetish. This
is hardly surprising given that the fetishist pays them hand-
somely. Being a scholar under fetishistic rule is more difficult.

Precisely because the fetishistic aspect of events is incomprehensible, the scholar mostly writes about their imperialistic and revanchist aspects. Historically speaking, many scholars who lived under fetishistic regimes were imperialists, but very few were fetishists. For various reasons, they did not approve of worship of the heel, and wrote critically about it. Most of them attempted to explain events as the product of comprehensible factors, either political or military; fetishism was subsumed within imperialism. It took courage to see brutal acts of genocide for what they were: senseless.

A mysterious feature of the Russo-Ukrainian War was the aggressor's use of the letter Z. At the very start of the invasion, it appeared on Russian tanks and other vehicles. Used as a symbol of war and a sign of support, the letter Z spread all over Russia. Patriots painted it on police cars, on the sides of buildings and on their clothing. In Kazan, children who were dying in a hospice were lined up in a Z formation for a macabre photo that was widely disseminated by state media. The war was being fought against the West – why then was a Latin letter, foreign to the Cyrillic alphabet, chosen as its symbol? Since there was no official explanation, the theories multiplied. Some said that the Z came from the Russian word *zapad*, which means "the west"; others said it stood for Zelensky and that Russian troops had been ordered to kill him. True believers saw in the Z one half of the swastika, which they claimed was an ancient symbol of the Slavs. Critics thought it was taken from zombie films. Whatever the truth, in the spring and summer of 2022 the Latin Z proliferated throughout Russian life and media.

There is a fetish beneath every genocide: circumcised flesh, the pronunciation of certain words, a tattoo. None of them justifies murder, and only a fetishist would disagree with this. But we know that the fetishization of such minor differences took place, and it cost millions of lives. With the Z, this spectacle of history took another step: since there were no words that could serve to differentiate friends from foes, a symbol had to be invented from scratch. Though entirely senseless, belief in the Z, love for the Z, identification with the Z, would identify a true patriot.

Putin's speech that launched the war

While the oppressor carries out his horrible acts independently of all reason, he is still committed to explaining himself to various audiences. The perpetrators do not justify their acts to their victims, but they do offer justifications to audiences at home and abroad. Here the choice of rhetorical formulas and tropes is important. With his collectivization program Stalin transformed the condition of the Ukrainian peasantry, which he saw as individualist and profit-centered, into the communitarian, ascetic and bureaucratic order of the "collective farm." For Putin, it was more difficult to decide upon a rhetorical strategy: first, there was no ideology to speak of, no understanding of the desired transformation; second, he had already declared that Russians and Ukrainians were one and the same people. How to organize a genocide when the new pattern was indistinguishable from the old?

Rhetorical strategies were available to Putin in the form of *four genocidal tropes*: 1) presenting the captured territory as *terra nullius*, a virgin land with no people or pattern to speak of; 2) presenting the current genocide as a symmetrical response to a *previous genocide* committed by the other side; 3) *distorting the memory* of the previous pattern so that the imposed order could be presented as new and different; and finally, 4) denigrating the previous order and *stretching the perceived differences* so that the planned changes would match the declared ambitions. These tropes are logically different, but they could be combined for practical purposes. In more traditional terms, each of them portrays the oppressed population in its own way. Respectively, they involve 1) denial, 2) revenge, 3) amnesia and 4) defamation.

Usually, efforts to deny, explain and justify a mass murder begin after it has taken place, but this time they started before or during the event itself. Putin's speech on February 24, 2022, screened as the war began, was an instance of such preemptive justification.[21] Guided missiles followed immediately after the broadcast. Pre-recorded, it was choreographed as the starting point of a quick assault, the success of which was considered a certainty by both the speaker and most of his listeners: the declaration of a war which the very people who believed victory to be certain were forbidden to call a 'war'.

The first half of Putin's speech was not about Ukraine at all. He discussed global history – World War II, NATO expansion and the "redivision of the world" that came with the end of the Soviet Union. The first specific topic Putin addressed was the NATO bombing of Belgrade, "a bloody military operation"; interestingly, he also avoided calling it a "war," employing instead the same elusive trope of "special military operation" he used for his own attack on Ukraine. Although "some Western colleagues [had] prefer[ed] to forget it," the bombing of Belgrade was lodged in Putin's memory so well that he used it to justify the bombing of Kyiv. He also described in detail the wars in Syria, Iraq and Libya, as well as related policies of the United States. The first half of his speech read not as a declaration of war on Ukraine but as a long and tedious lecture on US interventions in Europe and Africa. Ukraine was absent from the picture. The values the US had supposedly been aggressively imposing upon Russia were said to be "directly leading to degradation and degeneration, because they [were] contrary to human nature." Putin was effectively declaring war against the US and its allies, not against Ukraine. Ukraine was not even a proxy: it did not exist, it was a *terra nullius*. The US, said Putin, "sought to destroy our traditional values and force on us their false values that would erode us." This is Lemkin's definition in reverse. Initiating his genocide, Putin presented it as a case of victims taking revenge for a previous genocide, this one allegedly committed by the US against Russia. Ukraine was still not in the picture.

In the middle of the speech, Putin stated that the US had recently "crossed the red line" with threats against "the very existence of our state and its sovereignty." Only in this part of his speech did he explicitly mention genocide and Ukraine. "We had to stop that atrocity, that genocide of the millions of people who live [in Donbas]." This claim was outlandish: there were never millions of Russians in the Donbas region and no genocide ever took place there. But Putin repeated the claim again, now explaining the purpose of his operation: "to protect people who, for eight years now, have been facing humiliation and genocide perpetrated by the Kiev regime . . . to demilitarize and denazify Ukraine." The Russians and the Ukrainians are essentially the same, but some Ukrainians are Nazis and therefore different. But the Ukrainians have no agency; they have literally done nothing in this speech. The Americans had turned their Ukrainian friends into Nazis, the opposite of the Russians, who defeated Nazism and disliked the Americans.

Thus, Putin's speech proceeded from 1) *terra nullius* to 2) preemptive accusations of genocide to 3) distorting memories of the initial condition through historical manipulation to 4) exaggerating the extent of the ethnic difference and so of the required change. At the end of his speech, Putin reiterated his denials and euphemisms: "The current events have nothing to do with a desire to infringe on the interests of Ukraine ... They are connected with the defense of Russia from those who have taken Ukraine hostage." If Ukraine's national pattern had already been destroyed by the American-led genocide, the forthcoming Russian genocide would purge this Americanized pattern. Russia would rescue the true Ukrainian condition from all contaminations, replacing what was different with that which was similar.

Triangulating the differences by referencing the alleged American degradation of Ukraine was Putin's solution to the problem of small differences. His speech slid from the idea that there were no differences between the Russian and the Ukrainian national patterns to the idea that there were polar differences between them. But since these differences were the result of foreign influence, they could be purged for the sake of the original sameness. This state of unity was hidden, but it was the only true state. Those who had no agency could be killed without further notice. The survivors would return to their initial condition, in which Russians and Ukrainians were the same people. Others would have to die to redeem their "degradation and degeneration, because they are contrary to human nature."

8

Defederating Russia

The Russian Empire disintegrated at the end of an imperialist war. The Soviet Union collapsed at the end of the Cold War. What would happen to the Russian Federation? The answer was obvious, even if it saddened many.

I am not calling for the collapse of the Russian Federation. I am predicting it, which is by no means the same thing. Even for people like me, who looked forward to Ukraine's total victory and to seeing Russia's rulers tried at an international court, it was not easy to admit that the Russo-Ukrainian War spelled the end of the country. The collapse of this composite state had long been feared, but the Russian rulers succeeded in freezing their domain for a while. Reflecting this central concern of the regime, the ruling party went by the name "United Russia." Navalny called it "the party of crooks and thieves," but the name these people chose for their party articulated their fear of disintegration and lack of other values. They had a chance: a favorable economic situation and a competent government could have staved off the collapse. Their failure was not the work of foreign peoples or governments; before the war, Western governments had been the best allies of a "United Russia."

The era of empires was long gone. Russia called itself a federation, like Germany or Switzerland, but it was behaving like an empire in decline. Federations are defined by the free accession and secession of their members; Brexit is a good example. In contrast to historic empires such as Austria-Hungary, the USSR had a constitutional mechanism permitting its dissolution. The principle of self-determination was adopted by the Bolsheviks in November 1917 and enshrined in the Soviet constitution. The same formula of self-determination became the founding principle of the League of Nations, and later of the United Nations. But after the collapse of the Soviet Union, "the right of self-determination, including secession" disappeared from Russian constitutional texts. The principle, however, had not been forgotten.

Composite states and federations bring an added value to their peoples, a *federative premium*. Pursuing economy of scale and a politics of synergy, it is possible to keep this premium positive. This should be the central concern of any composite state, such as the European Union, the United Kingdom or Russia. In a parasitic petrostate that functions as a logistical hub for trading and redistributing its natural resources, the federative premium is negative (see Chapter 3). Political tradition, historical mythology or the imperial domination of one ethnicity over others can defer the collapse of this unproductive formation. Empires and federations develop in peace, consolidate in war and disintegrate after defeat. It would be better for them to remain pacifist like Switzerland, but they tend to be aggressive like Russia. In the way of nemesis, the wars they start are likely to be suicidal.

In describing this process, I prefer the term "defederation" to the more commonly used "decolonization," because the former implies a transformation of all parts of the composite state while the latter applies only to colonies and doesn't refer to the metropolitan core of the empire.[1] There was nothing predetermined in the process: if Russia had not invaded Ukraine it would probably have deferred or avoided its defederation. But revanchism proved stronger than caution, and fetishism stronger than reason.

Russian imperialism

As an empire, Russia emerged on the international stage at the same time as the early Portuguese and Spanish empires, grew in competition with great terrestrial powers such as Austria and China, matured in a race with the British and French maritime empires, and outlived most of them. In the seventeenth century, Moscow colonized the Urals and Siberia. In the eighteenth century, it annexed the Baltic lands, the Crimea, parts of Poland, and Alaska. In the nineteenth century, it took Finland, the Caucasus, parts of the Balkans, and Central Asia. Externally aggressive, the Russian Empire was a threat to revolutionary France and enlightened Prussia, to British India and Spanish California. Internally oppressive, the Empire crushed a major mutiny in the Urals, sparked several revolts in Poland, unleashed a permanent rebellion in the Caucasus, and confronted violent revolutions in its capitals.

The Empire was deeply integrated in European politics. Russian soldiers took Berlin in 1760, Paris in 1814 and Budapest in 1848, but they did not do it alone; every time, the Russian Empire was part of an international coalition. Founded as a military capital, St. Petersburg was also a center of diplomacy. Famous diplomats served there – Joseph de Maistre, John Quincy Adams, Bismarck. . . After the victory over Napoleon, Russian diplomats created the Holy Alliance, a first attempt to integrate Europe by marrying military prowess to conservative ideology. Always a hyperactive player, the Russian Empire extended its Big Games to Central Asia, North America and the Middle East.

The closest historical analogy to the Russo-Ukrainian War of 2022 is the Crimean War of 1853–56, which was lost by Russia. In his wartime dispatches to *The New-York Daily Tribune*, Karl Marx wrote that "a certain class of writers" attributed to the Emperor of Russia, Nicolas I, "extraordinary powers of mind, and especially of that far-reaching, comprehensive judgement which marks the really great statesman. It is difficult to see how such illusions could be derived."[2] Russia was never as isolated in its fight against modernity as in these two wars. In both, the Russian army's logistics were poor, its weapons obsolete, its morale low, and the generation gap between its soldiers and their political masters tremendous. In both, the anti-Russian coalition was stronger, though its aims were vague. In both, Russia's disinformation split Western pundits. As Marx wrote, "a lot of reports, communications, etc., are nothing but ridiculous attempts on the part of the Russian agents to strike a wholesome terror into the Western world."[3] Both wars challenged the internal structure of the Russian imperial state, and both led to a swift transition of power from the fathers to the sons, or even the granddaughters. In both, ethnic issues were important but not decisive. Close to the end of the Crimean War, the British government discussed a plan for a "war of nations," which would have involved supporting nationalist movements in the Caucasus and elsewhere so that the Russian Empire could be weakened and dismembered. The plan never came to fruition as the government in London fell, and Nicolas I died (or took his own life) at just the right time to not have to acknowledge his defeat. The new British government signed a toothless peace with the heir to the throne, Alexander II. He launched the Great Reforms of the 1860s – still the most successful attempt at modernizing Russia.

All Russian and Soviet reincarnations of the ancient Muscovite state were imperialist, but their successes were not consistent. For every expansionist tsar or commissar like Catherine II or Putin, there was a leader who presided over the contraction of the Empire's domains: Alexander II sold Alaska, Lenin withdrew from Finland and Ukraine, and Gorbachev gave away much more. None of them liked this part of the job, but I am not sure that matters. While imperial victories consolidated the conservatism of the state, military defeats led to reforms and revolutions. The Great Reforms followed defeat in the Crimean War; the revolution of 1905 followed defeat in the Russo-Japanese War; the two revolutions of 1917 responded to the catastrophe of World War I; and the dismembering of the Soviet Union in 1991 concluded the Cold War. The Soviet collapse led to the liberation of fifteen countries, including Ukraine and Russia. It was a great example of the peaceful transformation of an empire, and part of the success story of global decolonization. However, the Russian loss of territory was smaller than that experienced by the British or even the German empires when they lost their colonies. The large-scale violence that tends to accompany the end of empires was only deferred.

Revanchism

The word "Ukraine" means "the edge." Over the centuries, Ukraine's lands and peoples both absorbed Russian expansionism and limited it. A central target of Russia's colonizing efforts, Ukraine was forced to supply the Empire with its goods, services and cadres. While the Ukrainian Cossacks rebelled against Russian rule, the Ukrainian nobility participated in running the Empire, and Cossack strongmen were included in the imperial elite. Ruled from its distant corner, St. Petersburg, the Empire was ambitious and unstable. Its new Crusades to capture Istanbul, Jerusalem or Manchuria fueled Russia's military efforts up until World War I. With the Bolshevik revolution, the renamed empire lost some peripheric lands but preserved its core. The move of the capital to Moscow, the creation of the Soviet Union and its victory in World War II gave new energies to imperial expansion. After the war, the Soviet Union annexed parts of Bukovina, Eastern Prussia, the Baltic countries and Tuva. Parts of Ukraine and Moldova, and parts of the Pacific coast, changed their status more than once. Throughout the twentieth century, the Russian borders shifted almost as often as the most unsettled parts of the global South.

In 1991, as a newly independent country, Russia adopted a new constitution and dismantled the old power structures. Like the metropolitan center of any collapsed empire, Moscow experienced massive problems, including the loss of traditional markets, the disruption of supply chains and the frustration of the elite. At that point of bifurcation, Russia had two strategic options. The first was postcolonial development, which would have seen Russia bid final farewell to the Soviet state in exactly the same way the Ukrainians or Estonians did. A revolution had taken place and the new Russian laws, leaders and institutions had nothing in common with their Soviet predecessors. In this narrative, Russia was a colony of the Soviet Union in the same way as Latvia or Uzbekistan were. But this new country, post-Soviet Russia, was still a composite state. There was no reason to expect that, left to themselves, the constituent parts of the former empire such as Chechnya, Tatarstan or the oil-rich parts of Western Siberia would maintain their loyalty to Moscow. Left to its postcolonial humbleness, Russia would need to accept further splits and secessions. Indeed, local protests and rebellions began immediately after 1991. The other option was a continuation of the imperial narrative in which the Russian state was the exclusive heir to the Soviet Union: the survivor of a "geopolitical catastrophe," as Putin put it, the target of a global conspiracy and a bulwark against the apocalypse. One option was a decolonization of Russia, the other a reconquest of the original Soviet space. The former would promise peace and prosperity, the latter war and revanchism.

The choice was soon made. Vladimir Putin came to power in 2000 with the promise of suppressing a major rebellion in the Caucasus. Two bloody and wasteful Chechen wars (1994–96 and 1999–2009) undermined the project of democracy-building in Russia. Putin pressed further, depriving the constituent parts of the Federation of their sovereign powers (2013) and invading Georgia (2008) and Crimea (2014). With every imperial endeavor, Putin consolidated his personal rule. A basic truth of imperialism is that external expansion and internal oppression are connected like two sides of a coin.

In 1993, Galina Starovoitova warned about the dangers of a "Weimar Russia" – defeated, revanchist and crumbling. As she put it, "the secession of smaller republics would be less problematic for Russia than any attempt to keep such lands by force."[4] Five years later, Starovoitova, a brilliant ethnographer and arguably the most successful female politician in post-Soviet Russia, was murdered by a political assassin.

The biggest country in the world, the Russian Federation was "the subaltern empire," the "red mirror" of global troubles, a "failed state" on the brink of rupture.[5] Reconquering the Caucasus and Crimea that had belonged to the Soviet Union, the new Russia increasingly identified with Soviet might and glory. Each step towards reconquering Ukraine was a major step towards restoring the Soviet Empire. Unlike classical imperialism, which sought new lands and adventures, Putinism was a revanchism – a less common but particularly toxic kind of imperialism.

On its enormous territory, populated rarely and unevenly, the Russian Federation was fragile. Its population density, nine persons per square kilometer, was comparable to that of Finland or Canada. In these vast northern countries, people congregate in a small number of habitable nooks, leaving other areas thinly settled.[6] In the post-Soviet era of expensive transportation and relatively open borders, people toured and traded in adjacent lands more than in national centers. The men and women of Konigsberg (Kaliningrad) had better opportunities for studying, working or finding a partner in Poland or Germany than in central Russia. The same was true for the millions living in the agglomerations of Southern Siberia: they had better chances of getting on in life in China or Mongolia than in Russia. The Caucasus traded and prayed with Turkey, the White Sea coast traded with Norway, and St. Petersburg with Finland and northern Europe. Moscow was booming while the provinces were looking elsewhere. The very size of the country facilitated its disintegration.

In May 2022, during the third month of the Russo-Ukrainian War, the BBC Russian service produced an instructive study. Exploring data from eleven cemeteries with fresh military graves, the journalists identified more than 3,000 Russian soldiers killed in Ukraine and listed their hometowns. The results were stunning: the soldiers came from distant regions of Russia, and a majority of them were of non-Russian ethnicity. Dagestan suffered most of the losses, Buryatia ranked second, the Volgograd region third, followed by Bashkortostan and Southern Siberia. These were the poorest areas in the Russian Federation, plagued with high unemployment. The locals either volunteered to serve in the army or were unable to bribe their way out of obligatory service. Among the dead, there were only six (0.2 percent) from Moscow, even though the capital's residents accounted for 9 percent of Russia's population.[7] Putin was wary of declaring general conscription, fearing it would lead to mass protests in the capital. Partial mobilization was declared only in September, and it confronted the demographic and healthcare problems that Russia had suffered for decades (see Chapter 6). No province lost more from the war than Donbas, which consisted of two Ukrainian regions that had been controlled by Russian-sponsored separatists since 2014: their men were conscripted, and women fled to Russia having no support there. As Bruno Latour wrote, "there are the two pincer movements of the *land grab*: the one appropriates, the other excludes."[8]

Towards the beginning of his reign, Putin was asked what had happened to the Russian submarine *Kursk*, which perished in the Arctic in August 2000. "It sank," he said, with a cynical smile. The tautology of his response masked the shocking catastrophe. In trying to rescue the legacies of the Russian past – Orthodoxy, imperialism and Soviet collectivism – Putin wished to melt them into a new substance that could only be referred to as Putinism. But there was no melting pot for the task. It sank.

Ethnicity or politics?

The Russian economist Natalya Zubarevich spoke of the four belts of Russia: the first was made up of a dozen big cities, each with a population of more than a million; the second consisted of the decaying industrial belt of the Volga and the Urals; the third was the enormous agrarian heartland stretching from the Ukrainian border to the Pacific coast; and the fourth included the poor areas of the Caucasus and Southern Siberia, most of which were ethnically non-Russian.[9] The government redistributed revenues, and all four belts were beneficiaries of the transfers that came from a small number of internal colonies – the oil-pumping and gas-trading regions at the center of the Eurasian continent. The biggest donors were two "autonomous districts" named after their indigenous populations that were largely extinct: the Khanty-Mansi District and the Yamalo-Nenets region – a vast land of empty marshes and migrating reindeers in Western Siberia. Another donor was Moscow, the official residence of many extractive corporations that were drilling and mining in Siberia but paying taxes in the capital. Nevertheless, the Khanty-Mansi delivered so much and consumed so little that this region contributed two times more to the Russian budget than Moscow.[10]

Tatarstan was another breadwinner in the post-Soviet empire. Settled on the banks of the Volga River, this booming community possessed its own oil fields and industrial facilities. Speaking in Kazan, the capital of Tatarstan, in 1990, Boris Yeltsin offered the locals "as much sovereignty as you can swallow." Tatarstan held a referendum, and the citizens voted for sovereignty. Many debates about the elusive meaning of this word followed. In 1992, Moscow and Kazan signed a treaty, and Tatarstan became a "state united with the Russian Federation." However, its economic growth was faster than the rest of Russia's, and in many respects it acted like an independent state.[11] On coming to power, Putin declared an end to this "parade of sovereignties." In 2001, Tatarstan's referendum was retrospectively declared unconstitutional. Having already lost billions of dollars to Moscow, Tatarstan had now lost its political autonomy as well.

In 2017 this attack on Tatar sovereignty, or what remained of it, resumed. This time the target was culture and language rights: Kazan lost its power to teach the Tatar language in local schools. The number of people who identified themselves as Tatars was decreasing with every new poll: many felt it safer to declare a Russian identity. But in contrast to Chechnya, Tatarstan retained a relative prosperity and peace. Moreover, its officials supported the war in Ukraine and recruited ethnic troops to fight there. Other "republics" such as Bashkortostan, Chuvashia and Chechnya also created ethnic battalions with ethnic commanders. In the nineteenth century, the Russian Empire had supported such formations, but the Soviet Union shunned the practice on the grounds that it would feed nationalist violence and lead to the risk of new internal conflicts. In March 2022, émigré Tatar activists published an appeal urging the people of Tatarstan to separate from Russia.[12] Eventually, the fate of the Russian Federation would be decided in Kazan and the other capitals of the Eurasian republics, rather than in Moscow.

From Karelia to Chukotka, self-identified Russians had a numerical majority in many ethnic regions of Russia. However, confrontations between Moscow and the provinces concerned social and environmental issues as well as language and cultural policies. In this maze, Russians and non-Russians had many overlapping interests. The Russo-Ukrainian War demonstrated that, in the modern world, it is not ethnicity or identity that define people's choices but politics. Before 2014, Ukraine was a land of ethnic peace like Tatarstan, but it was forced to fight for its freedom like Chechnya. Many of those who fought in the Ukrainian army in 2022 spoke better Russian than their Russian foes, and made better use of their Soviet-manufactured weapons. Unlike homogeneous Chechnya, which is culturally distant from Russia but lost its war against the overwhelming force of Russian weapons and money, heterogeneous and culturally similar Ukraine was able to confront Russia vigorously.

The mass migration of Russians, Ukrainians and many others to Europe, Israel and the United States showed that these people could quickly become responsible citizens. As the Soviet saying had it, in their homeland they "pretended to work while their employers pretended to pay." In the US, ethnic Russians boasted median incomes that were higher than those of Chinese, Italian or even Swiss migrants.[13] One in four staff members at Israel's universities were native Russian speakers. The first generation of post-Soviet Russians who arrived in Israel surprised the locals with their right-wing views, but research showed that the voting preferences of the second generation were indistinguishable from those of the general population.[14] Multiple waves of Russian emigrants, including those who fled Putin's war in 2022, were natural experiments in causality. It was the Russian state that made its citizens of any ethnicity unproductive and frustrated, not the other way around.

Indigenous rights

Various nations in the Russian territory had been impatient with Putin's state. In 2019 in Izhevsk, the capital of the Udmurt Republic, Albert Razin set himself alight in protest at the suppression of his native Udmurt language. A banner found next to his body read "If my language disappears tomorrow, I am ready to die today" – a quote from the Dagestan poet Rasul Gamzatov.[15] Earlier, in 2013, Ivan Moseev, a leader of the Pomory (Seasiders), was arrested for "inciting hatred against Russians" and collaborating with the Norwegian intelligence services. Almost nine years later, the European Court in Strasbourg ruled against Russia, declaring Moseev the victim of an illegal verdict. The Pomory – an ethnic minority in the Russian North with a distinct identity and culture – spoke a dialect of the Russian language and had never experienced serfdom. Led by the Pomory, massive protests shook Shiyes, a village in the Arkhangelsk region, in 2018–20. This barely populated area had already been crisscrossed by eight gas and oil pipelines. Moscow planned to construct a monstrous landfill there, destroying the woods that the locals used for hunting and berry-picking. It would have been Europe's largest garbage dump, with waste delivered from Moscow, located 1,200 kilometers away.[16] The mass protests, in which locals blocked the railway line with tents, lasted two years. The project was cancelled in 2020. It was the biggest victory of the Green movement in contemporary Russia.

During the 1990s, indigenous rights were included in the new Russian constitution. The Russian Federation accepted responsibility for the "defense of age-old environments of habitation and traditional ways of life" (Article 72). The American political philosopher Leif Wenar argued that respecting the rights of indigenous peoples was the only way out of the oil curse: if hydrocarbons are to be mined and burned at all, the profits should go to the locals, and especially to those who have been discriminated against in previous periods.[17] As Wenar observed, the constitutions of almost all nations proclaim that local mineral treasures belong to the people. This formula was present in the Soviet constitutions, but it never appeared in the constitution of the Russian Federation. The habitats of the Khanty, Mansi, Yakuts and other indigenous peoples of Northern Eurasia were circumscribed to facilitate the extraction of oil, gas, coal and diamonds. Drillers destroyed even the national parks that had been created for these peoples in the 1990s. In 2017, Russian oil workers beat up Sergei Kechimov, a Khanty herder and shaman who tried to defend the holy Lake Numto from their invasion. Citing four oil spills that threatened local fish and birds, Kechimov tried to sue the powerful oil and gas company Surgutneftegaz, but was unsuccessful. Federal legislation passed in December 2013 removed the protected status of lands on which indigenous people hunted, fished and herded.[18] In 2019, Alexander Gabyshev, a Yakut shaman, set out for Moscow on foot, "to drive President Vladimir Putin out of the Kremlin"; he was arrested on the way and subjected to forced psychiatric treatment, a form of torture.[19] Even before the war, Marjorie Balzer, an American anthropologist who spent years in Yakutia, Buryatia and Tuva, believed in the potential of their emancipatory movements.[20] Intense discontent had been growing in the major cities of Siberia.[21] Booming industrial centers, they experienced a sharp decline when the military orders dried up, as had happened after the Cold War and as happened again after the Russo-Ukrainian War. In September 2022, mass anti-government protests occurred in Dagestan, against both conscription and the war itself.

Having visited St. Petersburg in 1839, in the wake of the Russian army's brutal suppression of yet another Polish uprising, the French author the Marquis de Custine wrote that the Russian Empire was an "enormous prison, and only its emperor had the keys." In 1914, Lenin called the Russian

Empire "a prison of nations." This cyclical narrative was to be disrupted.

Bullitt's attempt

A hundred years before the Russo-Ukrainian War, two revolutions and a bloody civil war plunged the Russian Empire into chaos. In March 1918, the Bolsheviks exited World War I, signing a separate peace treaty with the Central Powers at Brest-Litovsk, in which Russia pledged to supply oil, gold, timber and other commodities to Germany. The Allies were worried that the Germans would take over parts of Russia and seize resources in the Urals. To preempt this, Japan proposed to invade Russia before the German army did. Moving along the Trans-Siberian Railway, the Japanese troops would make their way up through Siberia to the Urals. The Americans opposed the plan. Nurturing a romantic affinity for Russia, Woodrow Wilson's administration feared a stronger Japan. If Japan occupied Siberia, what guarantee would there be that its troops would ever leave? The future showed that Japan was indeed an unreliable ally of America.

Negotiations on the issue were led by Edward House, Wilson's chief advisor on European politics during World War I and at the Paris Peace Conference. A Southerner who owned plantations and wrote novels, House was a permanent presence in Democratic administrations up until the eve of World War II. In 1918, Wilson and House diluted the Japanese invasion plan by limiting its force to 10,000 men. In the event, largely thanks to the US president and his advisor, the Japanese invasion never happened.[22]

World War I ended a few months later. But chaos continued to reign in Russia. Wilson had led his country into war in order to establish a perpetual peace. The Versailles Peace Treaty reshaped Europe, but the fire continued to blaze in Russia.

The various combatants in the Russian Civil War sent their representatives to the Paris Peace Conference. Their reports contradicted one another on each and every point. To clarify the situation, Wilson dispatched a reconnaissance mission to Russia.

William Bullitt, a young diplomat and journalist, led the mission, which also included two spies and one poet. The delegation was received in Moscow by Lenin, who enchanted Bullitt; as it happened, the sympathy was reciprocal. It was April 1919, when the Bolsheviks were at their most vulnerable: retreating, they controlled the least territory of all the combatants in the Civil War. Bullitt drew up a plan for reconciling all the belligerents. The former Russian Empire would be divided into twenty-three parts; each combatant would get the territory it controlled at that moment. Finland, Ukraine and the Baltic countries had already been recognized by the international community. Southern Russia, the Urals, Siberia and Tatarstan would also become independent states. The Bolsheviks would be left with Moscow, Petrograd and eight provinces surrounding these cities. The project fit with Wilson's concept of the self-determination of peoples. In a similar way, the Balkan states were created on the ruins of the Austro-Hungarian Empire. The arbiter would be a new international organization, the League of Nations, which would recognize the new independent states at a special conference in Oslo.

Lenin agreed to Bullitt's proposal and confirmed his participation in the planned conference. Now, Bullitt and House had only to convince the remaining combatants. But first the plan had to be approved by Woodrow Wilson. Bullitt rushed from Moscow to Paris, where House was preparing for a meeting with Wilson. The meeting never took place. The president was tired and had heart problems; probably he had his first stroke. But it is also possible that Wilson's hesitation was linked to his attitude towards Russia: he did not want to be responsible for its dismantlement.[23]

For Bullitt, this was a severe disappointment, and he resigned. He later went on to testify against Wilson in the Senate. House was also upset. He proposed as an alternative that Russia should be divided into five parts, with Siberia independent and European Russia split. Wilson was not convinced, and the peace plan failed again. Bullitt later wrote a psychobiography of Wilson, co-authored with Sigmund Freud. In it, he claimed with bitterness that Wilson's rejection of the plan to split Russia was "the most important single decision that he made in Paris."[24] Indeed, Wilson saved Russia twice – the first time from Japanese invasion, and the second time from internal secession.

On December 23, 2021, Putin reiterated his suspicion of American intentions towards Russia. He recalled that "one of President Woodrow Wilson's advisors" had endorsed the partition of Russia into five parts, and cited an entry in House's personal diary from September 1918. The Russian president did not, however, thank his American counterpart for having preserved a united Russia.

Who needed this Federation?

Much had changed in Eurasia since the era of Wilson and Lenin. Russia's military and economic power had impressed its neighbors for decades. Two key factors ensured this might: nuclear weapons, which provided security, and fossil fuel exports, which generated the enormous revenues that stabilized the local currency and enriched the rulers.

Neither was produced by the living generations. Oil was not created by labor; some places had it but many others did not, which was why it was so expensive. Russia's nuclear weapons had been built by the fathers or grandfathers of those in power. Relying on their pipelines and inherited nuclear umbrella, the Russian leaders appropriated the nation's wealth without lifting a finger. Embezzlement created record inequalities not seen even under the tsars. Two unearned privileges, wealth and security, shaped the elite that started the war. Well-paid propagandists assured the people that peace, tranquility and a stable currency were being secured through the hard work of this elite. The people believed this for as long as they had peace, tranquility and a stable currency. They thanked their leaders, and for a while it seemed as if these rulers would rule forever.

But for decades, nothing was produced in the Federation. The pipes continued to pump oil and the nuclear weapons continued to protect. The rulers got older and richer, and the people went on with their lives more or less without complaint. The Federation consisted of many regions, large and small, and they didn't complain either. Thanks to the oil, the money the elite received was convertible and could be used to buy nice cars or villas abroad. Thanks to the nuclear weapons, the Federation protected all its regions from their enemies and from each other. As long as there was peace and oil in the Federation, everyone could hope that this would always be the case. The oil would flow out through the pipes and the money would flow back in. The formidable weapons would continue to protect while remaining unused. There would be more and more villas and yachts to purchase overseas. And nothing too bad would happen to the ordinary folk.

The best-kept secret of the Federation was why its rulers decided to start their war. Explanations ranged from boredom to despair, realism to fetishism. More significant was the fact that the rulers had never waged such a war and were not expecting it to be a long and difficult endeavor. They did not know that during it their oil would no longer be purchased, that goods would stop flowing into the country, that people accustomed to having money would stop working if they were left unpaid. Confronting such difficulties, the rulers now had to decide whether to use their nuclear weapons.

On the one hand, if they were not used, the Federation would lose the war. There were many explanations for why they couldn't win without using these weapons: their commanders were incompetent, their missiles were imprecise, their soldiers were hungry. The fecklessness of the rulers was matched by the impotence of the people; both had been numbed by the constant flow of oil and the awesome power of their weapons. Now that the oil was no longer flowing, the weapons would have their say.

On the other hand, these ancient weapons of the ancestors had never been used. For decades they had sat in storage, their use-by dates extended many times. Of course, they had been tested, but over the months of war the rulers realized that drills were one thing and combat quite another. In short, using the nuclear weapons was a difficult decision to take. The Federation's rulers were not prepared to take it, or maybe their weapons were not in good shape. The soldiers fought to the bitter end until they lost the war.

Well, they lost and that's all there is to it. The rulers had to move on. But first they had to pay for the colossal damage they had done to their neighbor, and this used up all the reserves they had not already wasted. They were left with a lot of oil they couldn't sell and a lot of weapons they couldn't use. Discontent spread throughout the Federation.

The rulers' villas and yachts were gone. Their nuclear weapons had been feared only for as long as others thought they could be used against them. But since the Federation had lost its most important war without using its most important weapons, that meant it would never use them. And it would never sell oil again either: people abroad had somehow learned to live without oil. So who now needed this Federation?

Oil that could not be sold and weapons that could not be used turned the center of the country into an enormous warehouse for the dirtiest scum on earth. But in many other regions of the Federation, a new life began. Not immediately, but they gradually learned how to earn their own living and defend themselves. Some traded in the scraps the Federation had left them, but each eventually came up with their own ways to prosper: some sold grain, others cars; some taught students and others invited tourists. Relieved of the combined curse of oil and weapons, these were beautiful countries.

It was the people who decided which countries emerged after the Federation broke up. Ethnic tensions played their role, but events were triggered by the exhaustion of the subsidies and protection the regions had received from Moscow. Some of them already had their borders and leaders in place, others did not. New borders and authorities were contested, and violence followed. But it could not be worse than what the Federation had unleashed with its nuclear threats, global blackmail and transcontinental famine.

The new states were diverse – some democratic, others authoritarian. Their bigger neighbors were their main partners in trade and security. New tensions and dilemmas emerged. Would China shift its focus from Taiwan to Siberia? Would Eastern Prussia be viable as an independent state or would it merge with one of its neighbors? How would the poor, overpopulated republics of the Caucasus sustain themselves? And how would the reparations to Ukraine be divided?

The Federation's dismemberment threw up an enormous number of legal, strategic and economic questions. Settling borders, rebuilding trade and negotiating security arrangements took decades. Dealing with the legacy of the heinous war and creating new statehoods did not happen immediately. But the peoples of the former Federation learned how to make their own way. History continued, and the international community took note of the changes.

A peace conference was held, modeled after the Paris Peace Conference of 1918–19. A new Eurasian Treaty completed the work begun at Versailles a century earlier. From Ukraine to Mongolia, the neighbors of the new countries mediated the negotiations. More successful federations such as the European Union and the United States also played a part. The new countries remembered their long period of subservience to the Federation with contempt. Above all, they were grateful to the country that had defeated the Federation in the war.

Notes

Introduction

1 Tony Judt, *Postwar: A History of Europe since 1945*, Penguin, 2006.

2 For my analysis of Kant's response to the Russian occupation, see Alexander Etkind, "Kant's Subaltern Period: The Birth of Cosmopolitanism from the Spirit of Occupation," in *Cosmopolitanism in Conflict*, Palgrave Macmillan, 2018, 55–83.

3 Marc Bloch, "Reflections of a Historian on the False News of the War," *Michigan War Studies Review*, July 2013, https://www.mi wsr.com/2013-051.aspx

1 Modernity in the Anthropocene

1 Zygmunt Bauman, *Intimations of Post-Modernity*, Routledge & Kegan Paul, 1992, 179. Bauman started his career as an intelligence officer in the Internal Security Corps of socialist Poland, fighting with the Ukrainian insurgents in the late 1940s.

2 Ulrich Beck, *Risk Society: Towards a New Modernity*, Sage, 1992; Anthony Giddens, *The Consequences of Modernity*, Stanford University Press, 1990, and Giddens, *Politics of Climate Change*, Cambridge: Polity, 2009.

3 James Lovelock, "Gaia: The Living Earth," *Nature*, December 18, 2003: 769–70; Lovelock, *Gaia: A New Look at Life on Earth*, Oxford University Press, 2016; Bruno Latour, *We Have Never Been Modern*, Harvard University Press, 2012; Latour, *Facing Gaia: Eight Lectures on the New Climatic Regime*, Polity, 2017.

4 Beck, *Risk Society*; Latour, *Facing Gaia*.

5 Alexander Etkind, *Internal Colonization: Russia's Imperial Experience*, Polity, 2011.

6 Yakov Rabkin and Mikhail Minakov, eds. *Demodernization: A Future in the Past*, ibidem, 2018; Alexander Etkind and Mikhail Minakov, "Post-Soviet transit and Demodernization," *The Ideology and Politics Journal* 1 (2018): 4–13.

7 Anthony Giddens, *The Constitution of Society: Outline of the Theory of Structuration*, Polity, 1984.

8 Masha Gessen, *The Man without a Face: The Unlikely Rise of Vladimir Putin*, 2nd edition, Riverhead, 2022, xii.

9 David G. Lewis, *Russia's New Authoritarianism: Putin and the Politics of Order*, Edinburgh University Press, 2020; Greg Yudin, "The War in Ukraine: Do Russians Support Putin?," *Journal of Democracy* 33.3 (2022): 31–7.

10 Daron Acemoglu and James A. Robinson, *The Narrow Corridor: How Nations Struggle for Liberty*, Penguin, 2019.

11 Niklas Luhmann, *Trust and Power*, Wiley, 1979, 4.

12 Vladimir Shlapentokh, "Trust in Public Institutions in Russia: The Lowest in the World," *Communist and Post-Communist Studies* 39.2 (2006): 153–74; Geoffrey Hosking, *Trust: A History*, Oxford University Press, 2014; Alexay Tikhomirov, "The Regime of Forced Trust: Making and Breaking Emotional Bonds between People and State in Soviet Russia, 1917–1941," *Slavonic & East European Review* 91.1 (2013): 78–118.

13 Ulrich Beck, "World at Risk: The New Task of Critical Theory," *Development and Society* 37 (2008): 10.

14 Samuel A. Greene and Graeme B. Robertson, *Putin v. the People: The Perilous Politics of a Divided Russia*, Yale University

Press, 2019; Tatiana Kasperski and Andrei Stsiapanau, "Trust, Distrust and Radioactive Waste Management in Contemporary Russia," *Journal of Risk Research* 25.5 (2022): 648–65; Vladimir Gelman, *The Politics of Bad Governance in Contemporary Russia*, University of Michigan, 2022.

15 Ulrich Beck, "Climate for Change, or How to Create a Green Modernity?," *Theory, Culture & Society* 27.2–3 (2010): 254–66, quoted from 257.

16 Pey-Yi Chu, *Life of Permafrost: A History of Frozen Earth in Russian and Soviet Science*, University of Toronto Press, 2021; Susan Alexandra Crate, *Once Upon the Permafrost: Knowing Culture and Climate Change in Siberia*, University of Arizona Press, 2022; Joshua Jaffa, "The Great Siberian Thaw," *The New Yorker*, January 17, 2022; https://theglobalobservatory.org/2021/11/how-permafrost-thaw-puts-the-russian-arctic-at-risk

17 https://www.bbc.com/news/science-environment-62652133

18 Veli-Pekka Tynkkynen and Nina Tynkkynen, "Climate Denial Revisited: (Re) Contextualising Russian Public Discourse on Climate Change during Putin 2.0," *Europe-Asia Studies* 70.7 (2018): 1103–20.

19 For a similar argument, see Brian D Taylor, *The Code of Putinism*, Oxford University Press, 2018.

20 https://www.mk.ru/politics/2022/07/20/putin-poshutil-naschet-netradicionnykh-otnosheniy-na-zapade.html

21 Kay Rollins, "Putin's Other War: Domestic Violence, Traditional Values, and Masculinity in Modern Russia," *Harvard International Review*, August 3, 2022.

22 For different views on Russia's fascism, see Timothy Snyder, "Fascism, Russia, and Ukraine," *The New York Review of Books*, March 20, 2014; Snyder, "We Should Say It. Russia is Fascist," *The New York Times*, May 19, 2022; Marlene Laruelle, "So, Is Russia Fascist Now? Labels and Policy Implications," *The Washington Quarterly* 45.2 (2022): 149–68.

23 http://rg.ru/2004/04/26/Illarionov.html; https://euobserver.com/world/15207

24 Daniel Schulman, *Sons of Wichita: How the Koch Brothers became America's Most Powerful and Private Dynasty*, Hachette UK, 2014.

25 Alexander Etkind, *Tolkovanie puteshestvii. Rossiia i Amerika v travelogakh i intertekstakh*, NLO, 2022.

26 Alexander Gusev, "Evolution of Russian Climate Policy: From the Kyoto Protocol to the Paris Agreement," *L'Europe en Formation* 380.2 (2016): 39–52.

27 https://ria.ru/20150619/1078810271.html

28 https://www.rbc.ru/economics/26/07/2021/60fac8469a7947d1f4871b47

29 https://www.reuters.com/world/asia-pacific/putin-blames-european-energy-market-hysteria-green-transition-drive-2021-10-05

30 Andrei Shleifer and Daniel Treisman, "A Normal Country: Russia after Communism," *Journal of Economic Perspectives* 19/1 (2005): 151–74.

31 https://www.iep.ru/en/world-bank-updates-its-country-classification-by-gni-per-capita.html

32 https://atlas.cid.harvard.edu/rankings

33 https://en.wikipedia.org/wiki/List_of_countries_by_spending_on_education_(%25_of_GDP)

34 https://tcdata360.worldbank.org/indicators/h3f86901f?country=BRA&indicator=32416&viz=line_chart&years=2001,2021

35 https://worldpopulationreview.com/country-rankings/carbon-footprint-by-country

36 https://www.theglobaleconomy.com/rankings/happiness

37 https://www.indexmundi.com/g/r.aspx?v=24

38 https://www.theglobaleconomy.com/rankings/wb_political_stability

39 https://www.offshore-energy.biz/norway-shows-lowest-and-canada-highest-upstream-carbon-footprint-rystad-says

40 https://www.sipri.org/commentary/topical-backgrounder/2020/russias-military-spending-frequently-asked-questions; https://faridaily.substack.com/p/-20-?utm_source=%2Fprofile%2F80457290-farida-rustamova&utm_medium=reader2

41 https://www.wilsoncenter.org/blog-post/two-lean-years-russias
-budget-for-2018-2020

42 Alexander Etkind, *Nature's Evil: A Cultural History of Natural Resources*, Polity, 2021.

2 Petrostate

1 Fernando Coronil, *The Magical State: Nature, Money, and Modernity in Venezuela*, University of Chicago Press, 1997.

2 Eduardo Gudynas, *Extractivisms: Politics, Economy and Ecology*, Fernwood, 2021.

3 Etkind, *Nature's Evil*.

4 Marshall I. Goldman, *Petrostate: Putin, Power, and the New Russia*, Oxford University Press, 2008.

5 https://www.forbes.com/sites/arielcohen/2018/06/29/opec-is
-dead-long-live-opec/?sh=133baa92217a

6 Timothy Mitchell, *Carbon Democracy: Political Power in the Age of Oil*, Verso, 2013; Bruno Latour, "Agency at the Time of the Anthropocene," *New Literary History* 45.1 (2014): 1–18; Etkind, *Nature's Evil*.

7 Michael L. Ross, *The Oil Curse*, Princeton University Press, 2012.

8 Paul Krugman, *Rethinking International Trade*, MIT Press, 1994.

9 John Rawls, *A Theory of Justice*, Belknap Press, 1971.

10 https://static.rusi.org/RUSI-Silicon-Lifeline-final-web.pdf

11 https://www.kommersant.ru/doc/5357614

12 https://www.vokrugsveta.ru/articles/karta-kolichestvo-smertei
-na-dorogakh-v-god-id620885

13 https://www.rbc.ru/business/15/06/2022/62a325689a7947f6223
811e2

14 https://world-nuclear-news.org/Articles/Putin-suggests-Germa
ns-replace-nuclear-with-firewo

15 https://www.visualcapitalist.com/mapped-solar-and-wind-po
wer-by-country

16 Mitchell, *Carbon Democracy*.

17 Etkind, *Nature's Evil*, chapter 13.

18 Clifford G. Gaddy and Barry W. Ickes, "Russia's Dependence on Resources', in Michael Alexeev and Shlomo Weber, eds. *The Oxford Handbook of the Russian Economy*, Oxford University Press, 2013; for the opposite position on Russia's oil curse, see Daniel Treisman, "Is Russia Cursed by Oil?," *Journal of International Affairs* 63.2 (2010): 85–102.

19 Ross, *The Oil Curse*.

20 Jakov Mirkin, "Rost zolotogo zapasa v Rossii – dlinnyj trend," *Rossijskaja Gazeta*, October 28, 2018.

21 Felix Creutzig, "Fuel Crisis: Slash Demand in Three Sectors to Protect Economies and Climate," *Nature*, June 13, 2022.

3 Parasitic Governance

1 Hannah Arendt, *The Origins of Totalitarianism*, Meridian Books, 1958.

2 Ivan Krastev and Stephen Holmes, *The Light That Failed: A Reckoning*, Penguin, 2019.

3 Nataliya Gevorkyan et al., *First Person: An Astonishingly Frank Self-Portrait by Russia's President*, Hutchinson, 2000, 192.

4 Vache Gabrielyan, "Discourse in Comparative Policy Analysis: Privatisation Policies in Britain, Russia and the United States," *Policy and Society* 25.2 (2006): 47–75.

5 Gevorkyan et al., *First Person*, 192.

6 https://www.npr.org/transcripts/1097135961

7 Leon Trotsky, *Chto takoe SSSR i kuda on idet*, Grassi, 1938.

8 https://www.wsj.com/articles/SB984947892753855394

9 https://thebovine.wordpress.com/2009/08/09/in-1999-35-million-small-family-plots-produced-90-of-russias-potatoes-77-of-vegetables-87-of-fruits-59-of-meat-49-of-milk-way-to-go-people

10 Nancy Ries, "Potato Ontology: Surviving Postsocialism in Russia," *Cultural Anthropology* 24.2 (2009): 181–212.

11 https://www.kommersant.ru/doc/2166065

12 The first LNG exports from Russia started in 2017; see https://
www.oxfordenergy.org/publications/a-phantom-menace-is-rus
sian-lng-a-threat-to-russias-pipeline-gas-in-europe

13 https://www.proekt.media/guide/gazprom-aleksey-miller

14 https://ec.europa.eu/commission/presscorner/detail/en/IP_18
_3921

15 https://www.europarl.europa.eu/news/en/press-room/201904
02IPR34673/natural-gas-parliament-extends-eu-rules-to-pipel
ines-from-non-eu-countries

16 Gessen, *The Man without a Face*, xii.

17 Thomas Piketty, *Capital and Ideology*, Harvard University Press,
2021.

18 E. T. Gaidar, *Gibel' imperii: uroki dlia sovremennoĭ Rossii*, Astrel,
2012.

19 Maria Snegovaya, "What Factors Contribute to the Aggressive
Foreign Policy of Russian Leaders?," *Problems of Post-
Communism* 67.1 (2020): 93–110.

20 James C. Scott, *Domination and the Arts of Resistance: Hidden
Transcripts*, Yale University Press, 1990.

21 Alexander Etkind, Kacper Szulecki and Ilya Yablokov, "Petroleum
Conspiracies: How Russian Policymakers Seek Meaning in Oil
Price Volatility," *Beyond Market Assumptions: Oil Price as a
Global Institution*, Springer, 2020, 79–102.

22 https://tass.ru/politika/6408976?

23 https://www.bbc.com/news/world-europe-37109169

24 https://meduza.io/en/feature/2022/06/20/a-chance-for-revenge

25 Etkind et al., "Petroleum Conspiracies."

26 Etkind et al., "Petroleum Conspiracies."

27 https://www.transparency.org/en/news/countering-russian-kl
eptocrats-wests-response-to-assault-on-ukraine

28 https://en.rebaltica.lv/2022/03/who-are-the-people-from-pu
tins-inner-circle-with-properties-in-latvia

29 https://www.forbes.com/sites/giacomotognini/2022/03/05/a-gu
ide-to-all-the-outrageous-mansions-and-estates-owned-by-san
ctioned-russian-billionaires/?sh=4499a6772e0f

30 https://www.swissinfo.ch/eng/how-russian-sanctions-are-per meating-switzerland-s-luxury-sanctum/47642728

31 https://www.bloomberg.com/news/articles/2022-04-07/germa ny-s-yachtmaker-to-the-oligarchs-asks-who-its-customers-are

32 https://www.rferl.org/a/putin-navalny-superyacht-scheheraza de/31764751.html

33 Jared Diamond, *Collapse: How Societies Choose to Fail or Succeed*, Penguin, 2011.

4 The So-Called Elite

1 Juliette Cadiot, *La societe de voleurs. La protection de la proprete socialiste sous Stalin*, EHESS 2019; Piketty, *Capital and Ideology*, 581.

2 Abram Bergson, "Income Inequality Under Soviet Socialism," *Journal of Economic Literature* 22.3 (1984): 1052–99.

3 Piketty, *Capital and Ideology*, 596; Philipp Ther, *Europe since 1989*, Princeton University Press, 2016.

4 Ilya Matveev, "Measuring Income Inequality in Russia: A Note on Data Sources," *Russian Analytical Digest* 263 (2021): 5–11.

5 Filip Novokmet, Thomas Piketty and Gabriel Zucman, "From Soviets to Oligarchs: Inequality and Property in Russia 1905– 2016," *The Journal of Economic Inequality* 16.2 (2018): 189–223.

6 Piketty, *Capital and Ideology*, 578.

7 Credit Swiss, *Global Wealth Report 2022*, 31, at https://www .credit-suisse.com/about-us/en/reports-research/global-wealth -report.html

8 https://www.statista.com/statistics/1262949/countries-with-the -most-millionaires; https://en.wikipedia.org/wiki/List_of_U.S._s tates_by_the_number_of_millionaire_households

9 Dmitrii Nekrasov, https://www.facebook.com/dmitry.al.nekra sov; https://www.moscowtimes.ru/2022/05/30/naselenie-za-vs yo-zaplatit-pochemu-nesmotrya-na-sanktsii-u-putina-ne-konc hatsya-dengi-na-voinu-a20792

10 Semyon Kordonsky, *Resursnoe gosudarstvo*, Regnum, 2007.

11 Evgeny Gontmakher and Cameron Ross, "The Middle Class and

Democratisation in Russia," *Europe-Asia Studies* 67.2 (2015): 269–84.

12 Gontmakher and Ross, "The Middle Class and Democratisation in Russia."

13 Olga Kryshtanovskaya and Stephen White, "Putin's Militocracy," *Post-Soviet Affairs* 19.4 (2003): 289–306.

14 Maria Snegovaya and Kirill Petrov, "Long Soviet Shadows: The Nomenklatura Ties of Putin Elites," *Post-Soviet Affairs* 38.4 (2022): 1–20.

15 https://ria.ru/20221119/sobyanin-1832713301.html

16 Anders Aslund, *Russia's Crony Capitalism*, Yale University Press, 2019; Karen Dawisha, *Putin's Kleptocracy: Who Owns Russia?* Simon and Schuster, 2014.

17 Piketty, *Capital and Ideology*, 600.

18 Kenneth Arrow, Samuel Bowles and Steven N. Durlauf, eds. *Meritocracy and Economic Inequality*, Princeton University Press, 2018; Daniel Markovits, *The Meritocracy Trap*, Penguin, 2019.

19 John Maynard Keynes, *The Economic Consequences of the Peace*, Palgrave Macmillan, 2019.

20 https://www.wsj.com/articles/SB95738578060490250

21 Maxim Trudolyubov, *The Tragedy of Property: Private Life, Ownership and the Russian State*, Polity, 2018.

22 Seymour Martin Lipset, *Political Man: The Social Base of Politics*, Johns Hopkins University Press, 1963, 41.

23 Adam Przeworski et al., *Democracy and Development: Political Institutions and Well-being in the World, 1950–1990*, Cambridge University Press, 2000.

24 Shleifer and Treisman, "A Normal Country: Russia After Communism."

25 Daniel Treisman, "Economic Development and Democracy: Predispositions and Triggers," *Annual Review of Political Science* 23.1 (2020): 241–57, quoted 255.

26 David Shearman and Joseph Wane Smith, *The Climate Change Challenge and the Failure of Democracy*, Praeger, 2007.

27 Anthony Giddens, *The Politics of Climate Change*, Polity, 2009, 36.

5 The Public Sphere

1 Dan Healey, *Russian Homophobia from Stalin to Sochi*, Bloomsbury, 2017; Alexander Sasha Kondakov, *Violent Affections: Queer Sexuality, Techniques of Power, and Law in Russia*, UCL, 2022.

2 Sirke Mäkinen, "Surkovian Narrative on the Future of Russia: Making Russia a World Leader," *Journal of Communist Studies and Transition Politics* 27.2 (2011): 143–65.

3 https://www.chathamhouse.org/2022/02/why-minsk-2-cannot -solve-ukraine-crisis

4 Peter Pomerantsev, *Nothing is True and Everything Is Possible: Adventures in Modern Russia*, Faber & Faber, 2017.

5 See Maurizio Carbone, "Russia's Trojan Horse in Europe? Italy and the War in Georgia," *Italian Politics* 24 (2008): 135–51; Valerie Sperling, *Sex, Politics, and Putin: Political Legitimacy in Russia*, Oxford University Press, 2014.

6 https://euvsdisinfo.eu/figure-of-the-week-1-3-billion; Anton Shekhovtsov, ed. *RT in Europe and Beyond: The Wannabe Elite of the Anti-Elites*, Centre for Democratic Integrity, 2022.

7 https://www.themoscowtimes.com/2004/03/18/did-soros-final ly-exit-svyazinvest-a232281

8 https://www.opensocietyfoundations.org/voices/george-soros -future-europe-and-russia-open-societies

9 Gregory Asmolov, "The Disconnective Power of Disinformation Campaigns," *Journal of International Affairs* 71.1.5 (2018): 69–76.

10 https://www.theguardian.com/world/2014/apr/24/vladimir -putin-web-breakup-internet-cia; Andrei Soldatov and Irina Borogan, *The Red Web: The Kremlin's Wars on the Internet*, Perseus Books, 2017.

11 https://www.rferl.org/a/russia-yandex-trouble-sanctions-ukra ine/31769182.html

12 Samuel A. Greene, "From Boom to Bust: Hardship, Mobilization & Russia's Social Contract," *Daedalus* 146.2 (2017): 113–27.

13 E.g., Putin's friend, the Rector of the Petersburg Mining University, earned 195 million rubles in 2016, the Rector of the Presidential Academy 65 million, and the Rector of the Higher School of Economics 45 million. The salary of a professor was estimated at 100–200 thousand rubles: https://myslo.ru/news /mir/2017-12-03-minobrnauki-proverit-zarplaty-rektorov-na -adekvatnost

14 https://rg.ru/2022/06/02/obiavleny-rezultaty-vyborov-ran.html

15 https://web.archive.org/web/20161230022705/http://www.slate .com/articles/news_and_politics/cover_story/2016/05/the_thri ving_russian_black_market_in_dissertations_and_the_crusade rs_fighting.html

16 Daniele Fattorini and Francesco Regoli, "Role of the Chronic Air Pollution Levels in Covid-19 Outbreak Risk in Italy," *Environmental Pollution* 264 (2020): 114732; Myrto Kasioumi and Thanasis Stengos, "The Effect of Pollution on the Spread of COVID-19 in Europe," *Economics of Disasters and Climate Change* 6.1 (2022): 129–40.

17 https://www.themoscowtimes.com/2021/10/08/russias-corona virus-excess-death-toll-hits-660k-a75254

18 https://www.washingtonpost.com/world/europe/russia-covid -count-fake-statistics/2021/10/16/b9d47058-277f-11ec-8739-5c b6aba30a30_story.html

19 Anders Aslund, "Responses to the COVID-19 crisis in Russia, Ukraine, and Belarus," *Eurasian Geography and Economics* 61.4–5 (2020): 532–45.

20 https://www.centrumbalticum.org/files/5109/BSR_Policy_Brie fing_11_2021.pdf; see also Anna Temkina and Michele Rivkin-Fish, "Creating Health Care Consumers: The Negotiation of Un/ official Payments, Power and Trust in Russian Maternity Care," *Social Theory & Health* 18.4 (2020): 340–57.

21 Konstantin Platonov and Kirill Svetlov, "Conspiracy Theories Dissemination on SNS Vkontakte: COVID-19 Case,"

International Conference on Electronic Governance and Open Society: Challenges in Eurasia, Springer, 2020.

22 Olga V. Kruzhkova et al., "Vandal Practices as a Psychological Response to the COVID-19 Pandemic," *Changing Societies & Personalities* 5.3 (2021): 452–80.

23 https://www.dissernet.org/publications/medinskyi-plagiat.htm

24 https://meduza.io/news/2022/06/09/putin-petr-i-ne-ottorgal -zemli-on-ih-vozvraschal-na-nashu-dolyu-tozhe-vypalo-vozvra schat

25 Gevorkyan et al., *First Person*, 52.

26 Alexander Etkind, "Mourning and Melancholia in Putin's Russia: An Essay in Qualitative Mnemonics," in Ellen Rutten et al., ed. *Old Conflicts, New Media: Post-Socialist Digital Memories*, Routledge, 2013, 32–48.

27 Alexander Etkind, "Stories of the Undead in the Land of the Unburied: Magical Historicism in Contemporary Russian Fiction," *Slavic Review* 68.3 (2009): 631–58.

28 Viktor Shnirelman, *Koleno Danovo. Eskhatologiia I antisemitizm v sovremennoj Rossii*, BBI, 2017.

29 Masha Gessen, "The Mysterious Murder of Darya Dugina," *The New Yorker*, August 26, 2022.

30 Alexander Etkind, *Warped Mourning*, Stanford University Press, 2013.

31 Jan Matti Dollbaum, Morvan Lallouet and Ben Noble, *Navalny: Putin's Nemesis, Russia's Future?* Oxford University Press, 2021; Alexander Etkind, "Alexey Navalny: A Hero of the New Time," *New Perspectives* 30.1 (2022): 19–26.

32 Jussi Lassila, "Aleksei Naval'nyi and Populist Re-ordering of Putin's Stability," *Europe-Asia Studies* 68.1 (2016): 118–37.

33 https://www.washingtonpost.com/opinions/2022/09/30/alexei -navalny-parliamentary-republic-russia-ukraine

6 Gender and Degeneration

1 Carl Schmitt, *The Concept of the Political*, University of Chicago Press, 2008, 52.

2 https://www.mckinsey.com/industries/metals-and-mining/our
   -insights/why-women-are-leaving-the-mining-industry-and-wh
   at-mining-companies-can-do-about-it;   https://www.respons
   ibleminingfoundation.org/app/uploads/EN_Research-Insight
   -Gender-Inequality-June-2020.pdf

3 Alexander   Etkind,   "Petromacho,   or   Mechanisms   of
   De-Modernization in a Resource State," *Russian Politics &
   Law* 56.1–2 (2018): 72–85 (published in Russian in 2013). Cara
   Daggett authored a similar concept; see her "Petro-masculinity:
   Fossil fuels and Authoritarian Desire," *Millennium* 47.1 (2018):
   25–44.

4 Ross, *The Oil Curse*, chapter 4.

5 Alexander Etkind, "Introduction: Genres and Genders of Protest
   in Russia's Petrostate," in Birgit Beumers et al., eds. *Cultural
   Forms of Protest in Russia*, Routledge, 2017, 1–16.

6 Simon Smith Kuznets, *Population, Capital, and Growth*, W. W.
   Norton, 1973.

7 https://www.focaalblog.com/2022/04/26/susan-paulson-gender
   -aware-care-in-pandemic-and-postgrowth-worlds

8 https://www.cambridge.org/core/services/aop-cambridge-core
   /content/view/CB2D305CB18AFF14E93BB0EDAA3DDC84/S1
   474746419000058a.pdf/gender_gap_in_life_expectancy_in_rus
   sia_the_role_of_alcohol_consumption.pdf

9 Mark G. Field, "The Health Crisis in the Former Soviet Union:
   A Report from the 'Post-war' Zone," *Social Science & Medicine*
   41.11 (1995): 1469–78.

10 https://www.pewresearch.org/fact-tank/2015/08/14/why-the
   -former-ussr-has-far-fewer-men-than-women/#:~:text=The
   %20gender%20ratio%20in%20Russia,Soviet%20nations%20are
   %20similarly%20low;   https://knoema.com/atlas/Russian-Feder
   ation/topics/Demographics/Population/Male-to-female-ratio;
   https://statisticstimes.com/demographics/country/china-sex-ra
   tio.php#:~:text=Gender%20ratio%20in%20China&text=In%20
   2020%2C%20the%20sex%20ratio,701.08%20million%20females
   %20in%20China.

11 https://www.statista.com/statistics/1089814/russia-women-to-men-ratio-by-age

12 https://en.wikipedia.org/wiki/List_of_countries_by_life_expectancy#CIA_World_Factbook_(2022)

13 https://www.weforum.org/reports/global-gender-gap-report-2021

14 https://www3.weforum.org/docs/WEF_GGGR_2021.pdf

15 Ying Feng and Jie Ren, "Within Marriage Age Gap across Countries," *Economics Letters* 210 (2022).

16 Yulia Artemyeva, "Economic Dimensions and Legal Regulation of the Recovery of Alimony Obligations for the Support of Minor Children in Russia," *Journal of Eastern European and Central Asian Research* 8.4 (2021): 640–52.

17 https://rg.ru/2022/05/30/rg-publikuet-predvaritelnye-itogi-vserossijskoj-perepisi-naseleniia.html

18 Michele Rivkin-Fish, "Pronatalism, Gender Politics, and the Renewal of Family Support in Russia: Toward a Feminist Anthropology of 'Maternity Capital,'" *Slavic Review* 69.3 (2010): 701–24.

19 Alexander Mitscherlich, *Society Without the Father*, Tavistock, 1969.

20 Maurice Godelier, *Métamorphoses de la parenté*, Fayard, 2004.

21 David W. Shwalb, Barbara J. Shwalb and Michael E. Lamb, eds. *Fathers in Cultural Context*, Routledge, 2013; Jonas Radl, Leire Salazar and Héctor Cebolla-Boado, "Does Living in a Fatherless Household Compromise Educational Success? A Comparative Study of Cognitive and Non-Cognitive Skills," *European Journal of Population* 33.2 (2017): 217–42.

22 Jennifer Utrata, *Women without Men: Single Mothers and Family Change in the New Russia*, Cornell University Press, 2015, 17.

23 William C. Cockerham, "The Intersection of Life Expectancy and Gender in a Transitional State: The Case of Russia," *Sociology of Health & Illness* 34.6 (2012): 943–57.

24 Tanya Jukkala et al., "Economic Strain, Social Relations, Gender, and Binge Drinking in Moscow," *Social Science & Medicine* 66.3 (2008): 663–74.

25 Anatoly Vishnevsky, 'The Depopulated Superpower', *Russia in Global Affairs*, 3 (2003).

26 https://www.washingtonpost.com/wp-dyn/content/article/2008/10/03/AR2008100301976.html

27 Nicholas Eberstadt, "Russia's Peacetime Demographic Crisis," NBR Project Report, May 2010, 5.

28 Albert O. Hirschman, *Exit, Voice, and Loyalty: Responses to Decline in Firms, Organizations, and States*, Harvard University Press, 1970.

29 https://worldpopulationreview.com/country-rankings/happiest-countries-in-the-world

30 Anne Case and Angus Deaton, *Deaths of Despair and the Future of Capitalism*, Princeton University Press, 2020; Lawrence King, Gábor Scheiring and Elias Nosrati, "Deaths of Despair in Comparative Perspective," *Annual Review of Sociology* 48 (2022).

31 Sharon Horne, "Domestic Violence in Russia," *American Psychologist* 54.1 (1999): 55.

32 Olimpiada Usanova, "Russia's 'Traditional Values' and Domestic Violence," *Kennan Cable* 53 (2020).

33 Anna Andreeva, Nataliia Drozhashchikh and Galina Nelaeva, "Women's Rights and the Feminists' 'Dirty Plans': Media Discourses during the COVID-19 pandemic in Russia," *Affilia* 36.3 (2021): 319–35.

34 https://bataysk-gorod.ru/news/shestdesyat-protsentov-tridtsati letnikh-detey-v-nashey-strane-zhivut-s-roditelyami; https://74.ru/text/family/2021/07/31/70054088

35 Utrata, *Women without Men*, 126.

36 https://www.reuters.com/article/us-russia-military-shooting-idUSKBN29Q0WI; https://www.themoscowtimes.com/2019/11/06/they-warned-theyll-rape-me-russian-soldier-stands-by-mass-shooting-a68062

37 Françoise Daucé and Elisabeth Sieca-Kozlowski, eds. *Dedovshchina in the Post-Soviet Military: Hazing of Russian Army Conscripts in a Comparative Perspective*, ibidem, 2006; Maya Eichler, *Militarizing Men: Gender, Conscription, and War*

in Post-Soviet Russia, Stanford University Press, 2011; Alena Maklak, "Dedovshchina on Trial: Some Evidence Concerning the Last Soviet Generation of 'Sons' and 'Grandfathers,'" *Nationalities Papers* 43.5 (2015): 682–99; Françoise Daucé, "Dedovshchina after the Reform: Ethnicity as a Justification for Violence in the Russian Army," *Problems of Post-Communism* 61.2 (2014): 36–45; Karen Petrone, "Gender, Militarism, and the Modern Nation in Soviet and Russian Cultures," *The Routledge Handbook of Gender in Central-Eastern Europe and Eurasia*, Routledge, 2021, 196–204.

38　Ulrich Beck, "How Modern is Modern Society?," *Theory, Culture & Society* 9.2 (1992): 163–9, quoted from 167.

7　Putin's War

1　https://en.wikipedia.org/wiki/List_of_Russian_billionaires

2　Mikhail Anipkin, "Pokolenie lishnikh lidei: antropologicheskij portret poslednego sovetskogo pokoleniya," *Neprikosnovennyj zapas*, 2018.

3　https://www.ukrinform.ru/rubric-world/3442324-glava-minfi na-germanii-peredumal-otnositelno-pobedy-putina-v-ukraine .html; Liva Gerster, "You Do Not Want to Hear His Words," *Frankfurter Allgemeine*, March 28, 2022.

4　Adam Tooze, Chartbook 68, https://adamtooze.substack.com /p/chartbook-68-putins-challenge-to?s=r; see also his further clarifications in Chartbook 81, https://adamtooze.com/2022/02 /12/chartbook-81-permanent-crisis-or-black-earth-agro-giant -alternative-futures-for-ukraine

5　Katrina vanden Heuvel, "A Path Out of the Ukraine Crisis," *Washington Post*, February 15, 2022.

6　Thane Gustafson, *Klimat: Russia in the Age of Climate Change*, Harvard University Press, 2021, 13–15.

7　Niall Ferguson, "Putin's Ukrainian War Is About Making Vladimir Great Again," Bloomberg, January 2, 2022.

8　Niall Ferguson, "Putin Misunderstands History. So, Unfortunately, Does the US," https://www.bloomberg.com/opinion/articles/20

22-03-22/niall-ferguson-putin-and-biden-misunderstand-histo
ry-in-ukraine-war

9   https://euideas.eui.eu/2022/07/11/john-mearsheimers-lecture
-on-ukraine-why-he-is-wrong-and-what-are-the-consequen
ces/?fbclid=IwAR0hxr83lSBwJYFUcnSOmKLIS8CjnrFsBpEG5
G3sCrL5oksk6Vcl7Oy6ZYk

10 In 1989 Finland imported 94 percent of its oil from the USSR,
paying mostly by food and consumer goods; this trade was "particularly profitable." Pekka Sutela, "Finnish Trade with the USSR:
Why Was It Different?," BOFIT 7 (2005); https://euromaidan
press.com/2022/03/01/finlandization-was-malignant-for-finla
nd-and-it-might-be-even-worse-for-ukraine

11 https://www.bloomberg.com/news/articles/2022-04-04/deutsc
he-bank-ceo-sees-german-recession-if-russian-gas-cut-off

12 https://www.brookings.edu/blog/ben-bernanke/2015/04/03/ger
manys-trade-surplus-is-a-problem

13 Alexander Etkind, "Ukraine, Russia, and Genocide of Minor
Differences," *Journal of Genocide Research* (2022), https://doi
.org/10.1080/14623528.2022.2082911

14 Raphael Lemkin, *Axis Rule in Occupied Europe: Laws of
Occupation, Analysis of Government, Proposals for Redress*, The
Lawbook Exchange, Ltd., 2005, 79.

15 A. Dirk Moses, *The Problems of Genocide: Permanent Security
and the Language of Transgression*, Cambridge University Press,
2021, chapter 6; Etkind, *Internal Colonization*, chapter 5.

16 Etkind, "Ukraine, Russia, and Genocide of Minor Differences."

17 Viktor Shklovskii, *Zoo, or, Letters Not About Love*, Cornell
University Press, 1971.

18 Pål Kolstø, "The 'Narcissism of Minor Differences' Theory: Can
It Explain Ethnic Conflict?," *Filozofija i Društvo* (2007), https://
doi.org/10.2298/FID0702153K

19 Sigmund Freud, *The Future of an Illusion, Civilization and Its
Discontents, and Other Works*, The Hogarth Press, 1961, 114.

20 Michael Ignatieff, *Blood and Belonging*, BBC Books, 1994, 14.

21 "Transcript: Vladimir Putin's Televised Address on Ukraine,"

Bloomberg, February 24, 2022, https://www.bloomberg.com/news/articles/2022-02-24/full-transcript-vladimir-putin-s-televised-address-to-russia-on-ukraine-feb-24

8 Defederating Russia

1 For recent statements on this issue, see Alexander Etkind, "Defederating Russia," Desk Russia, April 18, 2022, https://en.desk-russie.eu/2022/04/18/defederating-russia.html; Michael Casey, "Decolonize Russia," *The Atlantic*, May 27, 2022.

2 Karl Marx, *The Eastern Question*, Sonnenchein, 1897, 396.

3 Marx, *The Eastern Question*, 36–7.

4 Galina Starovoitova, "Politics After Communism: Weimar Russia?," *Journal of Democracy* 4.3 (1993): 106–9, quoted from 108.

5 Viatcheslav Morozov, *Russia's Postcolonial Identity: A Subaltern Empire in a Eurocentric World*, Springer, 2015; Gulnaz Sharafutdinova, *The Red Mirror: Putin's Leadership and Russia's Insecure Identity*, Oxford University Press, 2020; Janusz Bugajski, *Failed State: A Guide to Russia's Rupture*, Jamestown Foundation, 2022.

6 https://rujec.org/articles.php?id=30166

7 https://www.bbc.com/russian/features-61638530

8 Bruno Latour, *After Lockdown: A Metamorphosis*, Polity, 2021, 112.

9 https://www.vedomosti.ru/opinion/articles/2011/12/30/chetyre_rossii

10 https://www.acra-ratings.ru/research/2302

11 Katherine E. Graney, *Of Khans and Kremlins: Tatarstan and the Future of Ethno-Federalism in Russia*, Lexington Books, 2009.

12 https://www.idelreal.org/a/31748114.html

13 https://en.wikipedia.org/wiki/List_of_ethnic_groups_in_the_United_States_by_household_income

14 https://ridl.io/israel-s-russian-speaking-minority-political-force-in-the-knesset

15 https://globalvoices.org/2019/09/16/a-professors-self-immo
    lation-puts-the-spotlight-on-the-fragile-future-of-russias-mino
    rity-languages

16 Daria Tereshina, "'Shiyes Is Our Stalingrad': Garbage Riots and
    Moral Outrage in Northwest Russia," https://www.eth.mpg.de
    /5353781/blog_2019_12_10_01

17 Leif Wenar, *Blood Oil: Tyrants, Violence, and the Rules That Run
    the World*, Oxford University Press, 2015.

18 https://www.theguardian.com/world/2017/mar/17/reindeer
    -herder-oil-excavators-siberia;   https://www.themoscowtimes
    .com/2015/08/18/russian-shaman-battles-oil-giant-over-sacred
    -lake-a49038

19 https://www.amnesty.org/en/latest/news/2021/09/russia-siber
    ian-shaman-who-marched-against-putin-is-indefinitely-confi
    ned-to-a-psychiatric-hospital

20 Marjorie Mandelstam Balzer, *The Tenacity of Ethnicity*, Princeton
    University Press, 2021.

21 Fiona Hill and Clifford G. Gaddy, *The Siberian Curse: How
    Communist Planners Left Russia Out in the Cold*, Brookings
    Institution Press, 2003.

22 Carl J. Richard, *When the United States Invaded Russia: Woodrow
    Wilson's Siberian Disaster*, Rowman & Littlefield Publishers,
    2012.

23 Alexander Etkind, *Roads Not Taken: An Intellectual Biography of
    William C. Bullitt*, University of Pittsburgh Press, 2017.

24 William C. Bullitt, "Foreword," in Sigmund Freud and William
    C. Bullitt, *Thomas Woodrow Wilson: A Psychological Study*,
    Houghton Mifflin, 1966.

Index

abortions 96–7
abuse of history 71, 77, 79–80, 106, 119
Academy of Sciences 72–3
agency 3, 7, 85, 104, 119–20
agriculture 12, 43–4, 94–5
alcohol 61, 94–5
Anthropocene 3–4, 10, 14, 23–4, 39, 67, 77
Arctic 11, 129
Arendt, Hannah 40
authoritarianism 11, 26, 64, 68, 74, 84, 109

babushka (grandmother) 98–101, 104
Bakhtin, Mikhail 1, 10
Baku 35
Balzer, Marjorie 133
Bauman, Zygmunt 3
Beck, Ulrich 9, 11, 101, 142, 156

Bloch, Marc 2
Braudel, Fernand 1–2
Bullitt, William 134–6
Buryatia 128, 133
Bykov, Dmitry 78

capital flight 30, 60–62
Caucasus 35, 56, 68, 123–4, 127–9, 139
causality 93, 106, 131
Chayanov, Alexander 1, 94, 98
Chechnya 46, 126, 130–1
Chubais, Anatoly 34, 41–2
Cirillo, Lanfranco 82
civil society 9, 40
climate 4, 7, 10–11, 17, 23–4, 64, 74, 106
   awareness 4, 13,
   change 7, 11–13, 17, 23, 64, 74, 106

denialism 7, 11, 14–17
and war 23, 106
coal 14, 17–18, 21, 31–5, 106
Cold War 19, 63, 89, 93, 108, 121,
125
collapse 6, 17, 49, 58–60, 89, 93,
121–2, 125
collective farms 43, 94, 117
colonization 6, 38, 49, 110–11,
122, 125
internal colonization, 6, 22,
26, 129
commoners 10, 42, 44, 57, 76–7,
81, 137
conspiracy theories 10, 15,
49–51, 67, 76, 126
constitution 57, 122, 126,
130–3
Coronil, Fernando 24
corruption 5, 9–11, 13, 17, 22, 38,
42, 47–9, 52, 56, 61–4, 73,
78–84, 95; *see also* capital
flight; elite; Navalny
Covid-19 11, 14, 61, 74–7, 83, 89,
91–2, 94, 97
Creutzig, Felix 39
Crimean War 102, 124–5

decarbonization 11, 16–7, 109
dedovschina, the grandfather
rule 100–1
defederation 121–3, 127, 130–4,
136–40
degeneration 38, 93–7, 118–20
deindustrialization 17, 31

democracy 5, 35, 63–5, 105,
127
demodernization 7–8, 40, 50
dependency by proxy 109
Donbas 51, 67, 119, 128–9
Dugin, Alexander 79

education 10–21, 29, 38–9, 46,
58, 62, 72–4, 87, 92, 110; *see
also* universities
elections 46, 64, 70, 96
elite 7, 10, 15, 18, 28–31, 37, 40,
49–52, 55–65, 73, 77–84,
103, 136–7
emissions 6, 9–18, 20–1, 32, 39,
75
emotions 9, 77–80, 92, 100; *see
also* fetishism
boredom 102, 137
despair 2, 40, 78, 83, 94–6,
100–2, 137
fear 71, 79, 87, 121
happiness 20, 29, 96
jealousy 60, 84
mourning 2, 79
energy transition 4, 10, 12–18,
33, 106
environment 11, 24, 48, 131–2,
estates (*sosloviya*) 57
ethnicity 5, 102, 112–13, 119, 122,
124, 128–32, 139
Evtushenkov, Vladimir 43
experts 5, 10, 12, 19, 42, 104–8
extraction 20, 25–8, 41, 45, 51,
58, 86, 133

false news 2, 67, 70, 76, 107
family 44, 61, 87–102
  and domestic violence 97
  and fatherlessness 92–3
  nuclear 87–9
  post-socialist 90, 92, 98–9
  and social services 98–9
  three-generational 99–101
  see also abortions, *babushka*,
    Maternal Capital Program
far right movements 7, 22,
  26, 53, 80, 131; *see also*
  Putinism
Fat Years 36, 59, 97, 103
Federal Security Service (FSB)
  14, 43, 45, 47, 50
federative premium 122
Ferguson, Niall 106–7
Finland 25, 89, 96, 107–9, 123,
  125, 127–8, 135, 157
Finlandization 108–10
flaring 12, 20
fossil fuel 5, 8, 13–22, 25, 31, 36,
  51, 65, 80, 105, 136
  its role in the Russian budget
    17–18, 25, 36, 38, 86, 129
Freud, Sigmund 113, 115, 136

Gaia 4–5
Gaidar, Egor 49–50
Gazprom 43, 45–8, 51–2, 66
gender 1, 7, 85–93; *see also*
  inequality
generation 2, 58, 72, 79, 92,
  98–104, 114, 124, 131, 136

genocide 6, 110–20; genocidal
  tropes 117–19
Germany 21, 34–6, 48, 51, 53,
  105, 108–10, 128, 134
Gessen, Masha 8, 48
Giddens, Anthony 7–8, 64
gold reserves 7, 38, 41
Goldman, Marshall 26
grain 30, 36, 43, 80, 95, 107,
  139
growth 4, 15, 20, 26–9, 37–9,
  44, 49, 60, 63–5, 91, 105,
  130
Gustafson, Thane 105

hazing 100–1, 155–6
health 19–21, 40, 58, 61, 74–7,
  89, 94–8
hidden transcripts vs. public
  displays 10, 50
Hirschman, Albert O. 96
Holodomor 80, 110
homophobia 12, 67, 87, 100
House, Edward 134
housing 41, 88–9, 98
Huevel, Katrina vanden 105
hydropower 33

ideology 11–13, 37, 117, 123; *see*
  also Putinism
Illarionov, Andrei 14–15, 63,
  95
imperialism 6, 12–13, 64–5, 68,
  115–16, 123–5, 127–9
indigenous rights 129, 132–4

inequality 1–3, 31, 41, 44, 46, 56–8, 60, 63–4, 86, 98
and Russian regions 56; *see also* gender
international rankings 19–21, 33, 72, 96
international trade 7, 13, 16, 25–6, 29–31, 36–8, 45, 51, 60–2, 86, 95, 108–10, 139
internet 69–71, 99
Iran 25, 33, 64, 95

Kant, Immanuel 2, 108, 141
katechon 77–81
Keynes, John Maynard 1, 63
Khanty 56, 129, 133
Khodorkovsky, Mikhail 45–6, 52
Koch brothers 14–15, 58
Konigsberg/Kaliningrad 2, 128
Kouprianov, Alexei 75
Krugman, Paul 29
Kudrin, Aleksey 38–9, 74
Kuznets, Simon 87

labor 18, 22, 25–30, 37, 40, 57–8, 64, 86, 105, 136
labor theory of value 22, 25, 40
Latour, Bruno 3–5, 28, 142
Lemkin, Raphael 110, 114, 157
Lenin, Vladimir 125, 133, 135–6
libertarianism 11–12, 15–16, 22, 41, 56; *see also* taxation
Lindner, Christian 105
Luhmann, Niklas 9

Marx, Karl 22, 63, 115, 124,
Maternal Capital Program 91, 96
Mearsheimer, John 107
media 14, 66–9, 71, 76, 116
paper media 66–71, 76
social media 70–1
television 46, 50, 52, 66–71
Medvedev, Dmitry 14–17, 39, 52, 82
Melnyk, Andrij 105
mercantilism 22, 26, 37–8
meritocracy 59, 63
methane 11–12, 20
middle class 30, 41, 44, 57–8,
migration 20, 37, 60, 62, 83, 91, 97–8, 131
military expenditure 27, 39
Mitchell, Timothy 28, 35, 145
Mitscherlich, Alexander 92
mobilization 60, 62, 91, 97, 128, 133
modernity 1, 3–8, 75, 96, 99–102, 110, 124
gaiamodernity 4–7, 9, 10, 25, 32, 64, 109, 115
paleomodernity 3–6, 9, 11, 25, 31–3, 64, 88
modernization theory 63–5
monopoly 27–9, 45, 47, 69
muckraking journalists 42, 46, 84

nationalism 37, 69
NATO 107, 118

natural gas 7, 12–18, 20–1,
  25–39, 43–8, 51, 57, 86,
  105–10, 129, 132–3
  and long-term contracts 45,
    48, 109
  and planned economy 45, 109
natural resources 4–6, 17, 20, 22,
  25–9, 37, 41, 45, 57, 60, 64,
  80, 122, 134
  and the resource-bound state
    25, 28–30, 85, 109
Navalny, Alexei 46–7, 52, 81–4,
  121
nemesis 2, 12, 27, 48, 80, 102,
  107, 122
Nemtsov, Boris 36
neoliberalism 16, 19, 27, 35
nooscope 51
normalization (in scholarship)
  19–22, 64, 106–7
Norway 25–6, 33, 38–9, 61, 128,
  132
novels 67, 78, 134
nuclear weapons 65, 106, 137–8

oil 7, 11–8, 20–40, 43–8, 56–62,
  64–6, 73, 81, 86–7, 95,
  105–8, 126–3, 136–9
  and geography, 129–30
  and the Russian budget 18, 25,
    36–8, 86, 129
  and labor, 86–7
  oil prices 27–33, 36, 50–1, 59,
    108–9
  see also petrostate

oligarchs/oiligarchs 7, 30, 43, 47,
  49, 52–3, 54–5, 62, 81–6,
  103
OPEC 26–7
Orthodox Christianity 37, 63,
  78–9

palaces 47, 52, 82
Paris Peace Conference 134–5,
  139
pensions 17, 21, 38, 88, 90, 99
permafrost 11–12, 31
petromacho 86–7; see also
  gender
petrostate 24–31, 37–9, 51, 64,
  87, 95, 122
  and deindustrialization 17,
    31–4
  and magic 24, 50
  and monopoly 27–8
  and oil export 26–9
Piketty, Thomas 56, 147–8
pipelines 6, 11, 35–6, 45, 48, 52,
  59, 86, 107, 109, 116, 132
plagiarism 73–4, 77
Poland 70, 123, 128, 141
Polanyi, Karl 1
political realism 107, 137
pollution 4, 9–12, 75
Pomory 132
postwar 2, 35, 92
poverty 58, 98; see also
  inequality
predictions 106–8
Prigozhin, Evgeny 48

privatization 41–7, 58–9
  of apartments, 41
  loan-for-shares scheme 42, 69
  vouchers 41–2
progress 3–4, 6, 29, 33, 40, 109
Przeworski, Adam 64
public sphere 6, 10, 25, 29, 58,
    60, 62–84, 96, 101, 105, 109
  public goods vs. public bads 6,
    30–1
Putin, Vladimir 3–4, 11–14, 18,
    22, 30, 33–4, 41–3, 46–8, 51,
    53, 58, 68, 70, 77–85, 95–6,
    102–7, 114, 117–19, 124–30,
    136
Putinism 12–13, 16, 45, 78,
    100–2, 127

Qatar 21, 25, 27, 57

race 6, 110–11, 113–14,
Rand, Ayn 15, 63
Rawls, John 31
reflexivity 5, 10, 13–14
renewable energy 6, 33–4, 110
revanchism 13, 115–16, 123,
    125–7
revolution 5, 9, 14, 19, 32, 35, 62,
    71, 80, 87, 94, 123, 125–6,
    134
risk society 5, 141
Rosneft 47, 50–1, 60
Ross, Michael 28–9, 86–7,
    145–6
ruble 35–8, 95–7, 108

Russian Empire 35, 57, 59, 78–9,
    106, 121–7, 130, 133
Russian Federation 39, 56, 59,
    74, 121–2, 127–40
Russo-Ukrainian War 1, 3–4,
    8–14, 18–23, 32–4, 43, 51–3,
    60–2, 71, 77–80, 85, 91–2,
    97, 102–8, 114–20, 124,
    128–34, 137–40

sanctions 12, 32, 39, 52, 61, 71,
    95
Saudi Arabia 17, 20–1, 25–6, 64
Schmitt, Carl 8, 49, 63, 79, 86,
    152
Scott, James 10
Sechin, Igor 43, 47, 51, 53, 60
self-fulfilling prophecies 10, 71
Sharov, Vladimir 78
Shklovsky, Victor 111
Shleifer, Andrei 42–3, 64
Siberia 11–13, 20, 26, 31, 34–7,
    46–7, 50, 57, 75, 80–3, 95,
    97, 100, 110–11, 123, 126,
    128–9, 133–6, 139
Smash and Vengerov (pop
    group) 82
Sorokin, Vladimir 78
Soros, George 46, 69, 74
Soviet Union 3, 11–15, 26, 31–6,
    41–6, 49–50, 55, 58–60, 66,
    73, 76, 78, 88–9, 93–8, 100,
    103, 108, 121–7, 130, 133
Stalin, Josef 35, 42, 55, 78, 80,
    103, 112, 117

Starovoitova, Galina 127, 158
state, the 3–9, 20, 24, 26–30,
    38–41, 48, 58, 62, 81; *see
    also* petrostate
composite state 121–2, 126
failed state 105, 127
parasitic state 40–1, 122
resource-dependent vs. labor-
    dependent state 28–31
stopmodernism 1, 7, 9, 67, 71, 76
structuration 5, 7–8, 114
subsidiary plots 44
Surkov, Vladislav 67–8

taste 5–7, 13, 81–2, 85,
Tatarstan 35, 126, 130–1, 136
taxation 22, 28–30, 36, 44, 48,
    56–7, 63, 95, 129
tax evasion 49, 56, 82
terra nullius 117–19
Tooze, Adam 105
Transborder Carbon Tax 18
Tregub, Sergei 47–8
Treisman, Daniel 64, 144, 146
Trotsky, Lev 5, 42
trust 9–11, 60, 71, 76–7, 94, 96

Ukraine 1, 3, 7–8, 13–5, 19, 21,
    23, 27, 32–3, 46, 48, 50–1,
    62, 68–71, 77–9, 84–7, 91,
102–15, 118–22, 125–31,
    139–40
unearned money 64–5, 137
universities 31–2, 42, 71–4, 131
utopia 5–6, 26, 80
Utrata, Jennifer 93, 154

vaccines 76–7
Venezuela 24–6, 37, 47, 64, 95
vices 102
    arrogance 10, 65
    greed 22, 65, 87, 102,
    poshly 82
    sloth 87, 94
vanity 52–3, 82, 137
Vishnevsky, Anatole 86, 94, 155

waste 9–11, 20, 132
Weber, Max 4
Wenar, Leif 132–3, 159
Williams, Robbie 81–2
Wilson, Woodrow 134–6

yachts 30, 34, 43–4, 53–5, 82,
    137–8
Yeltsin, Boris 36, 130

Z (letter) 115–17; *see also*
    fetishism
Zubarevich, Natalya 129